# HOW TO RECOGNIZE THE ANTICHRIST

# HOW TO RECOGNIZE THE ANTICHRIST

## Arthur E. Bloomfield

BETHANY FELLOWSHIP, INC.
Minneapolis, Minnesota

Published by Bethany Fellowship, Inc.
6820 Auto Club Road, Minneapolis, Minnesota 55438

Printed in the United States òf America

*Library of Congress Cataloging in Publication Data:*

Bloomfield, Arthur Edward, 1895-
    How to recognize the Antichrist.

    1. Antichrist. I. Title.
BT985.B55        236        75-29424
ISBN 0-87123-225-1

# Contents

# Introduction

As this is being written, there are no signs of Antichrist in evidence, yet there are many people who think they can point to a certain man and say he is Antichrist. These people evidently have no conception of the Bible Antichrist. There are in that respect two Antichrists: (1) The popular conception of who he is and what he is like, which is almost universally held but which has little connection with Scripture. (2) The Bible Antichrist.

We must consider all aspects of this subject. Every detail of Scripture concerning this man must be fulfilled. A partial fulfillment of any prophecy is not a fulfillment at all. Therefore we must consider Antichrist in all his relationships. The Bible is our only source of information. The first step in the process of recognizing Antichrist is to know what the Bible has to say about him. That will be the main burden of this book.

We will quote much scripture. This book is based on the Bible, not on a vision. The Bible is a finished book. God says in Revelation, "For I testify unto every man that heareth the words of the prophecy of this book, If any man shall add unto these things, God shall add unto him the plagues that are written in this book" (Rev. 22:18).

As the author of this book I have no information not found in the Bible. God has given me no additional visions. I have tried to present the Scriptures in an easy-to-read format. I believe that the Bible is certainly more thrilling and illuminating than anything that can be said about it.

## CHAPTER 1

# Antichrist's Character and Names

Antichrist is an important subject of prophecy in both the Old and the New Testaments. He connects with all three of the main lines of prophecy; namely, the nations, the Jews and the church. Very little prophecy can be fulfilled before his coming.

Antichrist connects with the nations. Daniel is the book that deals specifically with the rise and fall of world empires, including the one that is to come. Daniel saw the future of the world empires in four visions. He starts with his own time —the Babylonian Empire—and carries the story all the way to the final empire under Antichrist. When Daniel comes in his visions to the final stages of world history, he deals almost exclusively with a man, the man we call Antichrist. As an example of the importance of Antichrist in Daniel's visions, we might cite his second vision found in the seventh chapter. The chapter has 28 verses; the first seven deal principally with the empires that are past, and most of the rest of the chapter is concerning Antichrist.

Antichrist will play a large part in the return of the Jews. In that respect Hitler was a prototype of Antichrist. The return of the Jews is in three parts, each one involved in a crisis. Hitler was involved in the first crisis which restored some of the Jews to their land. Antichrist will be the instigator of the second crisis, which will cause the Jews to repent and turn to God. Antichrist will also be the instigator of the third crisis, called Armageddon, when the armies of the world will be mobilized against Jerusalem, just before the Great Judgment Day begins.

Antichrist will eventually destroy the church. There will be no general or sustained persecution at the start, and possibly not for some years, but in the end Antichrist will turn against the church. There is very little prophecy concerning the nations, the Jews, or the church that can be fulfilled before the coming of the Man of Sin.

It would seem that Antichrist would be easily recognized, for nothing comparable to him has ever before appeared in the world. Many of his activities will be in the realm of the miraculous; even his coming will be mysterious. His accomplishments will be such as the world has never seen before. Almost any man today who reaches a place of power or popularity is thought to be Antichrist by some gullible souls.

Yet when Antichrist actually arrives, it would seem that at the beginning almost nobody will recognize him as such. His coming is after the working of Satan, and the wicked world will be completely fooled. This is indicated in a number of prophecies: "Let him who hath understanding count the number of the beast." He will deceive everyone except those who know their Bibles. The names given to him in the Bible will not be the names he uses, and only those who have spiritual understanding will associate the Bible names with his names. The Bible names indicate the real nature and work of Antichrist.

Antichrist will be a man, a satanic man, and a great deceiver. Paul says his coming is after the working of Satan with all power, and signs, and lying wonders.

The biggest single factor in the rise of Antichrist is deceit. When the disciples asked Jesus, "What shall be the sign of thy coming and of the end of the age?" the first thing He said was, "Take heed that no man deceive you, for many shall come in my name saying, I am Christ, and shall deceive many." Jesus was not referring so much to Antichrist himself as He was to the many false christs who would accompany Antichrist. This deceit is deceit on a grand scale.

When Paul wrote to the Thessalonians concerning the Second Coming of Christ, the first thing he said was, "Let no man deceive you by any means."

When in Revelation Antichrist is revealed, it says, "And the great dragon was cast out, that old serpent, called the Devil, and Satan, which deceiveth the whole world" (12:9).

Therefore, deceit is the major factor in the rise of Antichrist. The whole world will be fooled. The only defense against deceit is knowledge. People who know cannot be deceived. It is extremely important to know how to recognize Antichrist. At the start he is not coming as Antichrist but as the savior of the world.

Both Jesus and Paul, when they mention deceit, are talking about deceit among those who call themselves Christians, or who are connected with the church. An apostate church will be almost totally deceived. This is going to be the most tremendous and universal program of deceit ever perpetrated on the world. It will be worthy of Satan's cunning, probably his masterpiece. When Paul says that Antichrist is coming with all power, he does not leave out much that will be desired by Satan.

We who are Christians may know the facts and watch them develop with interest rather than with fear.

World conditions are now only starting to get bad; they will become much worse. Wise men are making some dire predictions, but only Bible prophecy has the answer. The answer revolves around a man, so the subject "How to Recognize Antichrist" is a most important study. This will become more and more apparent as we approach a world crisis.

Concerning the coming crisis Jesus warned, "Be not terrified," indicating that this crisis will have some terrifying features. Any threat of a world war would be terrifying because so many irresponsible nations have atomic capability. Some of our news commentators have warned us that Russia is now in a position to destroy this country. Any war anywhere in the world today could be the spark that would set off the conflagration. It is the atomic bomb that gives the terrifying aspect to any threat of war. I do not believe there will be an atomic war, but the threat of it will be terrifying. We will deal with this in more detail when we discuss the world conditions that will produce Antichrist. It will look as if nothing or no one can survive. This will be Satan's grand opportunity to take over the world.

All predictions not based on Bible prophecy will fail; this time only God has the answer.

Antichrist is not the solution to the world's problems; he will only seem to be. That is where the deception comes in. Actually he will leave the world in worse shape than he found it, even though for a time he may seem to have great success.

The final solution to the world's problems is not Antichrist, but Christ. The world's problems are so complex that only God has the solution. Antichrist is Satan's man, but Christ is God's man. Satan produces nothing but destruction; Christ will bring redemption. The world's problems will be resolved, but only after the coming of Christ. He is the Saviour and Redeemer.

The redemption process involves more than the saving of a comparatively few people whom we call Christians. It involves everything God created and called good. We shall have a new heaven and a new earth "wherein dwelleth righteousness." The new heaven and the new earth do not necessitate a complete destruction of the old, but rather a redemption of the old. As Paul said concerning himself after his redemption, "Old things are passed away, behold, all things are become new."

The world will pin its hopes on Satan's man, but the real hope of the world is Christ and His coming again:

ISAIAH 9

6 For unto us a child is born, unto us a son is given: and the government shall be upon his shoulder: and his name shall be called Wonderful, Counsellor, The mighty God, The everlasting Father, The Prince of Peace.

7 Of the increase of his government and peace there shall be no end, upon the throne of David, and upon his kingdom, to order it, and to establish it with judgment and with justice from henceforth even for ever. The zeal of the Lord of hosts will perform this.

A large part of the Bible is prophecy. There are over 200 prophetic subjects dealt with in the Bible. These prophecies are not all fulfilled at the same time. There is a succession of events, conditions, developments, and institutions.

Some prophecies seem to contradict each other. That is because they are concerned with different times. A prophecy applied to the wrong time is always a misunderstood prophecy. Sometimes it almost seems as though some teachers or writers on prophetic subjects simply take a lot of prophecies, put them into a hat and shake them up, and then arrange them according to their own fancy. This may be sensational at the time, but it is not conducive to a long-term understanding of the prophetic program.

The time involved for the fulfillment of the major prophecies concerning the end time could cover a whole generation. During that length of time, world conditions may undergo very great changes. The rise of Antichrist is the subject of one of these changes. It is not the first prophecy to be fulfilled, neither is it the last one. Prophecies which concern our subject must be placed in their proper order. Even though prophecy may seem to be fulfilled, if the other prophetic conditions are not in evidence, we do not have a scriptural fulfillment. So the first step in recognizing Antichrist is to put him in his proper place chronologically.

Current events and world conditions which cause the rise of Antichrist must of necessity come before his rise, so our first step in recognizing Antichrist is to recognize conditions which produce him.

### His Names

Antichrist is a man and will have a man's name. It is not revealed in the Bible. Therefore, none of the prophets knew his given name or his surname. However, in order to identify him, they give him many different names which we will now consider.

Antichrist is the subject of much prophecy which looms large in the book of Daniel and in the book of Revelation.

Each term they use to identify him has a special significance which must be taken into consideration if we are to make a correct identification. The term "Antichrist" comes entirely from First and Second John, and that is the first name we will consider.

## Antichrist

The prefix "anti" has two different meanings. It may mean "like" or "similar to." This meaning has been applied to the term "antichrist," and therefore it has been supposed by many that he will be like Christ, and the world will worship him because they think he is Christ. Actually, if the world thought that he was Christ, they would be more likely to crucify him than to worship him. In none of the references to Antichrist in the Bible is this meaning in view.

The term "antichrist" is taken from First and Second John, and it would be better to use the term in the meaning found in those references. In John, Antichrist is not like Christ, but is one who is opposed to Him.

### I JOHN 2
22 Who is a liar but he that denieth that Jesus is the Christ? He is antichrist, that denieth the Father and the Son.

In this same chapter:

18 Little children, it is the last time: and as ye have heard that antichrist shall come, even now are there many antichrists; whereby we know that it is the last time.

In these verses John recognizes the fact that

there is to be an Antichrist, a special individual who will be *against* Christ.

The fact that there are many antichrists in the world, according to John, indicates that this is the dispensation that will produce Antichrist.

In John the prefix "anti" means *against,* which is the usual meaning. Daniel says that "he shall also stand up against the Prince of princes" (Dan. 8:25). Antichrist will be against Christ and everything that pertains to Christ, such as the church and the Jews.

His opposition to the Jews will be apparent at the start, but his opposition to the church may take a different form. There will be no general persecution at the start.

### *The Little Horn*

Daniel has a number of names for Antichrist. The first one is "the little horn." A horn is Daniel's symbol for a king or ruler (we could include dictator), and also the country over which he rules. The Jews did not crown their kings; they anointed them. The anointing oil was carried in a horn, so when the oil was poured over the head of the new king, there would seemingly be a horn on his head.

Daniel makes no distinction between the king and the kingdom; the country and the head of the country are indicated by the same symbol. Although this little horn will stand up against the Prince of Princes—that is, Christ—"he shall be broken without hand"—his end will come by an act of God.

### *A Raiser of Taxes*

Daniel refers to Antichrist as a raiser of taxes. This may not be a name, but it is important as an identifying mark. The whole verse reads:

### DANIEL 11

20 Then shall stand up in his estate a raiser of taxes in the glory of the kingdom: but within few days he shall be destroyed, neither in anger, nor in battle.

An ancient manuscript reads: "He shall cause an exactor [assessor] to pass over, to the restoration of the kingdom."

There is a sense in which the Roman Empire will be restored. When a man acquires the power to tax, he has restored the empire. At the time of the birth of Christ, a decree went out from Caesar Augustus that all the world should be taxed. That would be the Roman world. When that happens again, Antichrist will have come.

Eventually Satan will take over the body of Antichrist so that he will actually be Satan in the flesh; when that happens, Daniel refers to him as "a vile person."

### The Assyrian

In Isaiah, Antichrist is called "the Assyrian." Therefore, prophetically his empire would be called Assyria. This is another way of saying that the Assyrian was a type of Antichrist and Assyria was a type of his empire.

Isaiah says (30:30, 31): "And the Lord shall cause his glorious voice to be heard, and shall shew the lighting down of his arm, with indignation of his anger, and with the flame of a devouring fire, with scattering, and tempest, and hailstones. For through the voice of the Lord shall the Assyrian be beaten down, which smote with a rod" (rather, *with the rod will Jehovah smite—Pulpit Commentary*).

This has all the elements of the plagues sent

upon the kingdom of the Beast and his final destruction as recorded in Revelation and elsewhere.

Isaiah 10 is a remarkable portrait of Antichrist as the enemy of the Jews. Almost every verse has a parallel in some other part of the Bible. It is the story of the time when the Assyrian becomes God's rod to bring the Jews to repentance (Isa. 10:24). It refers to the covenant with Antichrist which Daniel foresaw (Dan. 9:27).

Antichrist is always the enemy of the Jews, but God will use him to bring them to repentance.

### ISAIAH 10

5 O Assyrian, the rod of mine anger, and the staff in their hand is mine indignation.

6 I will send him against an hypocritical [profane, R.V.] nation, and against the people of my wrath will I give him a charge, to take the spoil, and to take the prey, and to tread them down like the mire of the streets.

7 Howbeit he meaneth not so, neither doth his heart think so; but it is in his heart to destroy and cut off nations not a few.

He does not mean to be God's rod. He does not mean to bring the Jews to repentance. He intends only to destroy them. Antichrist's relationship to Israel is not that of a messiah, false or otherwise; but rather that of an enemy.

## Gog and Magog

Ezekiel associates Satan with Antichrist and refers to them as Gog and Magog. Gog is Satan, and Magog, the earthly representative of Satan. Here Satan and Antichrist are very closely associated as they are in Revelation.

## The Chaldean

Habakkuk uses the same method of identifying Antichrist. He uses the name of an ancient or con-

temporary conqueror who has characteristics
similar to those of Antichrist. He calls him the
Chaldean and gives his reasons. The Chaldeans
were a "bitter" and "hasty" nation.

## The Man of Sin

Jesus does not give Antichrist a name, but refers to him over and over again. Paul calls Antichrist the man of sin, and says his coming into
power will be engineered by Satan.

## The Beast Out of the Sea

Revelation calls Antichrist the Beast out of the
sea. Here a symbol is used for a name. The symbol
is a beast which rises out of the sea, the sea being
a symbol of the masses of people. In Revelation
a beast is an empire or the head of one.

These names all indicate that Antichrist will
be primarily a dictator or ruler whose ambition
is to conquer the world.

The territory actually conquered or ruled by
Antichrist will be limited roughly to Bible lands,
primarily the Roman Empire, but eventually ex-
tending across the Middle East. This will give Antichrist sufficient power so that he can dictate terms
of prosperity to the whole world. How he will do
this is told in quite some detail in the Bible. It
has been supposed by some that Antichrist will
be a false Messiah and that the world will worship
him because they think he is Christ. Some say
that he will be a pope. Others say he will be a
Jew. There is no scriptural foundation for these
assertions.

There are two kinds of dictators: One is primarily the head of a church who craves worldly
power and wants to rule as king; the other is primarily a ruler or conqueror or dictator who wants
to be worshipped. Such a man was Hitler. Antichrist will be like Hitler, not like a pope.

## CHAPTER 2

# The Resurrection

Many responsible people believe that we are at the end of the entire era—the immense upheaval of its demise is not yet foreseen by most people. It will exceed by far the upheavals of any previous end of an era.

The Bible does not mention the end of an era, but it does mention the end of the age. The disciples asked Jesus, "What shall be the sign of thy coming, and of the end of the age?" An era may be considered a shorter time than an age, but the end of an age could also be the end of an era.

According to Bible prophecy, Antichrist will be the dominant figure of the end of the age. In the beginning he will seem to save the world from universal disaster. Therefore we shall need to know: (1) What event marks the end of the age? (2) What are the signs leading up to this event?

The event we refer to is called the Rapture. "Rapture" is not a Bible word, but it is used to describe a Bible truth. It is the first event in the process called the "Second Coming of Christ."

The Second Coming of Christ is a process beginning with the resurrection and ending with the return of Christ to the earth to set up His Kingdom. Inasmuch as the resurrection is the first event in this process, it is the hub of the prophetic wheel. All prophetic events or conditions either lead up to the resurrection or proceed from it.

Jesus rose from the dead as He said He would. His resurrection is celebrated every Easter by the entire Christian Church. All the followers of Christ will also be raised from the dead in due time. Christians look forward to a new life. Paul said:

I CORINTHIANS 15

19 If in this life only we have hope in Christ, we are of all men most miserable.

20 But now is Christ risen from the dead, and become the firstfruits of them that slept.

21 For since by man came death, by man came also the resurrection of the dead.

22 For as in Adam all die, even so in Christ shall all be made alive.

23 But every man in his own order: Christ the firstfruits; afterward they that are Christ's at his coming.

The followers of Christ in the Bible are called "saints." Christ, we are told, will come with His saints. They will return with Christ and will be with Him when He sets up His Kingdom. If they are to come with Christ when He comes again, they must already be in heaven before that time, so the resurrection must come first. The Bible gives a very complete rundown on what will happen before the resurrection and what will happen between the resurrection and the Second Coming of Christ. We might diagram it as follows:

Now we come to a problem. At the time the dead in Christ are raised, there will be Christians living who belong in the company of them who are raised. They will never die, but will simply

## SECOND COMING

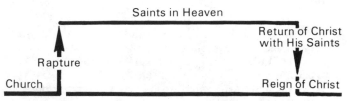

Saints in Heaven
Return of Christ with His Saints
Rapture
Church
Reign of Christ
Tribulation and Judgment

be changed and caught up to heaven in their new immortal bodies. We call this whole process the Rapture.

### I CORINTHIANS 15

51 Behold, I shew you a mystery; We shall not all sleep, but we shall all be changed,

52 In a moment, in the twinkling of an eye, at the last trump: for the trumpet shall sound, and the dead shall be raised incorruptible, and we shall be changed.

### I THESSALONIANS 4

15 For this we say unto you by the word of the Lord, that we which are alive and remain unto the coming of the Lord shall not prevent [precede] them which are asleep.

16 For the Lord himself shall descend from heaven with a shout, with the voice of the archangel, and with the trump of God: and the dead in Christ shall rise first:

17 Then we which are alive and remain shall be caught up together with them in the clouds, to meet the Lord in the air: and so shall we ever be with the Lord.

This is as plain as any words could make it. The first grand event that marks the end of this age is the resurrection of the dead in Christ and the changing of the Christians that remain alive.

Concerning those who are alive at that time, Jesus said:

MATTHEW 24

40 Then shall two be in the field; the one shall be taken, and the other left.

41 Two women shall be grinding at the mill; the one shall be taken, and the other left.

42 Watch therefore: for ye know not what hour your Lord doth come.

## The Reasons for the Rapture

Why does the Rapture have to take place at a certain time and why do all the saints of God have to be taken from the earth?

The Rapture is not only a turning point for the saints, it is a turning point for the world. The world will never be the same after the Rapture. Throughout the whole Bible there are predictions of a coming judgment on the world for its iniquity. Judgment is not only to punish the wicked, but to cleanse the world from the results of sin, and eventually to redeem it and perfect it so that we shall have a new heaven and a new earth "wherein dwelleth righteousness." That is a big order and cannot be accomplished without violence.

There have been judgments before. The flood of Noah's time changed the whole topography of the earth and established a climatic pattern which we still have today. Jesus said that there is coming a time of affliction such as never was since creation, or ever would be again (Mark 13:19). In the Old Testament this time of judgment is called the Day of the Lord.

The Day of the Lord is in two parts. The first part, a period of 3 1/2 years, is concerned mostly with the salvation of those who will accept Christ. There will be judgment, severe judgment, but its purpose will be the salvation of souls. Then will come seven years of judgment whose purpose is the cleansing of the earth from unrighteousness. Sometimes the prophets distinguish between these two periods by calling the second period the Great Day of the Lord or the Great and Terrible Day of the Lord. The prophet Zephaniah gives us a clear picture of the Great and Terrible Day of the Lord.

### ZEPHANIAH 1

14 The great day of the Lord is near, it is near, and hasteth greatly, even the voice of the day of the Lord: the mighty man shall cry there bitterly.

15 That day is a day of wrath, a day of trouble and distress, a day of wasteness and desolation, a day of darkness and gloominess, a day of clouds and thick darkness,

16 A day of the trumpet and alarm against the fenced cities, and against the high towers.

17 And I will bring distress upon men, that they shall walk like blind men, because they have sinned against the Lord: and their blood shall be poured out as dust, and their flesh as the dung.

18 Neither their silver nor their gold shall be able to deliver them in the day of the Lord's wrath; but the whole land shall be devoured by the fire of his jealousy: for he shall make even a speedy riddance of all them that dwell in the land.

The distress in the Great Day of the Lord is not caused only by natural circumstances such as earthquakes, volcanoes, hurricanes, and the like. They are sent from heaven and are administered by God's agents. Revelation records it in these words:

### REVELATION 8

7 The first angel sounded, and there followed hail and fire mingled with blood, and they were

cast upon the earth: and the third part of trees was burnt up, and all green grass was burnt up.

8 And the second angel sounded, and as it were a great mountain burning with fire was cast into the sea: and the third part of the sea became blood;

9 And the third part of the creatures which were in the sea, and had life, died; and the third part of the ships were destroyed.

10 And the third angel sounded, and there fell a great star from heaven, burning as it were a lamp, and it fell upon the third part of the rivers, and upon the fountains of waters;

11 And the name of the star is called Wormwood: and the third part of the waters became wormwood; and many men died of the waters, because they were made bitter.

12 And the fourth angel sounded, and the third part of the sun was smitten, and the third part of the moon, and the third part of the stars; so as the third part of them was darkened, and the day shone not for a third part of it, and the night likewise.

13 And I beheld, and heard an angel flying through the midst of heaven, saying with a loud voice, Woe, woe, woe, to the inhabiters of the earth by reason of the other voices of the trumpet of the three angels, which are yet to sound!

This is a judgment because of sin, but those who believe in Christ have been delivered from their sins; and God does not send judgments for sin on people who have been redeemed from their sins by the blood of Christ.

### JOHN 5

24 Verily, verily, I say unto you, He that heareth my word, and believeth on him that sent me, hath everlasting life, and shall not come into condemnation [judgment], but is passed from death unto life.

Therefore, God must remove His people from the earth before He can send the judgments.

Jesus refers to this same thing when He said to Martha:

### JOHN 11

25 I am the resurrection, and the life: he that believeth in me, though he were dead, yet shall he live:

26 And whosoever liveth [at that time] and believeth in me shall never die.

Satan is very much involved in the Day of the Lord. He has been at war with God ever since the Garden of Eden, and has been in virtual control of the world ever since. In the temptation of Christ, Satan offered Him all the nations of the earth. If Satan had not had these nations to give, it would not have been a temptation. Jesus did not challenge Satan's ability to deliver the nations.

This battle of the earth will reach its climax at the Rapture. At the time of the Rapture Satan will be cast out of heaven and down to the earth and will take up his abode in the body of a man and will reign here on earth in person till the coming of Christ. If Satan is to take over the body of a man at the time of the Rapture, then that man has to be here before the Rapture. That is the man we call Antichrist. You do not want to be here when Satan reigns.

You do not have to be here during the Great and Terrible Day of the Lord. A way of escape has been provided. Jesus said that it would be as it was in the days of Noah. In the days of Noah a flood was impending, but God warned Noah far enough in advance so that he could build an ark of safety and save himself and his family from the judgment which was coming.

Also, in the days of Lot God found that He had

to destroy the city of Sodom because of its iniquity; but before doing so, He sent His angel to deliver Lot and his family out of the city just before its destruction. Jesus said that it would be as it was in the days of Lot.

God allows His people to pass through times of calamity that come from natural causes brought on by either nature or man. These calamities are not judgments for sin. God allows them and then makes all things work together for good to them that love Him. But when God purposes to punish the world for its iniquity, He will first remove His people from the earth; so the Rapture has to come before these judgments strike. The reason for the Rapture is to save God's people from the day of calamity which is coming on the earth. At the end of the Day of the Lord Satan will be bound and cast into the bottomless pit.

## After the Rapture

After the Rapture everything changes quite suddenly. There is a change in the spirit world unseen by man, and that change in the spirit world is the cause of a great change on earth. Satan's all-out attempt to prevent the resurrection will result in his being cast out of his vantage point in the heavens down to the earth. Revelation puts it in these words:

REVELATION 12

7 And there was war in heaven: Michael and his angels fought against the dragon; and the dragon fought and his angels,

8 And prevailed not; neither was their place found any more in heaven.

9 And the great dragon was cast out, that old serpent, called the Devil, and Satan, which deceiveth the whole world: he was cast out into the

earth, and his angels were cast out with him.

10 And I heard a loud voice saying in heaven, Now is come salvation, and strength, and the kingdom of our God, and the power of his Christ: for the accuser of our brethren is cast down, which accused them before our God day and night.

It is not easy to comprehend exactly what this change means. Ever since creation Satan has been operating from heaven. He accused Job before the throne of God, and Revelation says he will accuse the saints one by one and attempt to prevent their resurrection. He is the great spiritual adversary.

At the Rapture all this will change. Satan will be cast down to the earth "having great wrath because he knoweth he hath but a short time." Satan's first project after being cast out of heaven is to obtain a body. He cannot create one; he can only possess one. The body he will possess is that of Antichrist. Antichrist will be killed in a mysterious way. Daniel says "neither in anger nor in battle." Revelation says it will be a sword wound. Satan will bring this man back to life to the amazement of the whole world. This will not be done in secret. God has just raised the dead; Satan will show that he can do the same thing.

Satan will put his own life into Antichrist. This is as close as Satan can come to an incarnation. Antichrist will be both man and Satan, yet Satan has also his own individual identity. In this way Satan achieves a counterfeit of God, being a trinity. This trinity is expressed in Revelation as the dragon (Satan), the beast (Antichrist), and the false prophet (the beast out of the earth). The trinity cannot be adequately explained in human words. Revelation says:

REVELATION 13

18 Here is wisdom. Let him that hath under-

standing count the number of the beast: for it is
the number of a man; and his number is Six hundred threescore and six.

The number six may be very prominent in the
name, nature, and work of Antichrist, even before
the Rapture. It is an identifying mark, but it is
not too evident. It requires some special knowledge
of Bible prophecy. It is not as simple as merely
substituting numbers for letters in a man's name.

How much of this 666 will be in evidence before the Rapture we are not told—quite possibly
all of it because it will identify Antichrist to the
believers, and after the Rapture the fact of Antichrist will be no secret to anyone. It is then that
he is revealed as Satan, and it is then that he
starts a great persecution of the believers. There
will be no question then as to the identity of Antichrist. After the Rapture there will be many false
christs and false prophets who will, if possible,
deceive the very elect who have been convinced,
convicted, and saved because of the Rapture.

*"Let him that hath understanding count the
number of the beast."* The beast is Antichrist in
Revelation. He operates both before and after the
Rapture. It may be that the Rapture itself will
reveal some of the identifying marks, but it is
when Antichrist first comes on the scene that it
is essential to recognize him. After the Rapture
there is no question about him. When the world
worships him, they will know they are worshipping
Satan: "They worshipped the dragon which gave
power unto the beast." In other words, they will
worship Satan who gives power to Antichrist.

Paul calls this the revelation of the Man of
Sin. When Antichrist is revealed as Satan, the identifying marks will become perfectly apparent. Everything changes at the Rapture. Before the Rap-

ture look for peace and prosperity and the building of great cities. Antichrist will undoubtedly be considered the greatest man who ever lived. He will captivate the world.

At the Rapture God will take peace from the earth. If God is going to take peace from the earth, there will have to be peace on the earth. After the Rapture Antichrist will fight many great wars. The only reason given as to why the people will worship him at that time is his ability to make war: "And they worshipped the beast, saying, Who is able to make war with him?"

It is very important that we recognize the great difference that comes over the world at the Rapture. If we are looking for the signs that will come after the Rapture, we may be greatly deceived, for those signs will not come at the start. Before the Rapture Antichrist will be a man of peace; after the Rapture he will be a man of war. It will be easy to count his number after the Rapture, but only those who have spiritual insight will be able to get his number when he first arrives on the scene.

*"His number is the number of a man."* This is a positive identification, although we may all be reluctant to apply it to this man when he is doing so much for the peace and comfort of the world. Make no mistake. This man will deceive the whole world, except those who have special insight. It will be difficult to point to so magnificent a benefactor and say he is Antichrist. If this book is not published before Antichrist arrives, it will probably be difficult to get it into print or into the stores.

*"His number is 666."* Revelation was written in Greek. The Greeks did not use the Arabic system of numbers, with numbers 1 to 9 and zero.

The numbers were written in letters; the letters of the alphabet had numerical values similar to our Roman numerals. It may be only after Satan has taken over that the entire trinity of sixes will be in evidence. This is all very mysterious and confusing. It is so designed that only the Holy Spirit can reveal it.

The Greek reads, "That is the number of man [not *a* man]," meaning that although the man claims to be God, and in the end is revealed as a trinity, his number is the number of man, not the number of God. It is not three ones; it is three sixes.

Many attempts have been made to substitute numbers for letters in a man's name and see if they add up to 666. Pages might be filled with lists of persons whose names have been proposed. Among the persons supposed to be indicated are a number of Roman emperors, Mahomet, Martin Luther, John Calvin, and Napoleon Bonaparte. The *Pulpit Commentary* suggests some rules whereby you can make any man's name add up to 666. They are: first, try it in Hebrew; if that does not work, try it in Greek; if that does not work, try Latin. If that does not work, add a title. If that does not work, do not be too particular about the spelling. Despite the irony, this is exactly what many people have done in trying to identify Antichrist.

## CHAPTER 3

# The Building of Great Cities

Ezekiel, in harmony with Revelation, brought together Satan and Antichrist in one process. He calls Antichrist the Prince of Tyrus; and Satan, the King of Tyrus.

Antichrist will be the builder of great cities. Although this feature may not be apparent at the start, as time goes on after the appearance of this man and the world becomes more and more entranced with his power, ingenuity, and greatness, the signs indicating that he is Antichrist will become more and more apparent to those who know the prophecies.

Two cities, Babylon and Tyre, are described in detail in prophecy. The third city to be built about the same time is Jerusalem, including the temple, although Jerusalem probably will not be built by Antichrist. It may even be built in spite of Antichrist; in fact, the time is coming when the Jews will have the upperhand in Israel and will demonstrate the possession of a power greater than Antichrist's. The visible symbol of that power will be the ark of the covenant.

Prophecy does not describe the building of

Babylon and Tyre. In each case the prophecy describes the destruction of the city, but in so doing it indicates how great the city is. A city has to be built before it can be destroyed; in fact, it has not only to be built, but exist and be lived in for some time. This is a factor concerning those times that should not be overlooked. We are not dealing with a single event, but rather with a long series of events, some of which at certain times seem to contradict all prophecies. There is one limiting factor: everything has to take place in the lifetime of one man.

Tyre will have to be rebuilt because it was never destroyed in the manner described by the prophet. There never was a city having the grandeur and worldwide importance of Tyre. There was a city of Tyre in the time of Christ, for we are told that Jesus went up to the coast of Tyre and Sidon. Tyre was destroyed, it is true, but not in the manner described by Ezekiel. Such a worldwide catastrophe could not have escaped the pages of history.

Tyre was actually two cities and will be again. There is an island in the Mediterranean Sea just offshore from Tyre. The people of the ancient city of Tyre built a city on the island for the sake of safety. When Tyre is finally destroyed, it will be by a great tidal wave coming down from the north, but this is a long time in the future, and it is not involved as far as the recognition of Antichrist is concerned. The destruction of Tyre is of interest to us now only because in describing its destruction, the prophecy indicates the greatness of the city which Antichrist will build. This picture painted by Ezekiel is so vivid that no words of mine could improve upon it. The only thing that should be noted is that the prophet had to call the future places by their ancient names, but the places mentioned covered almost all the known world of that day.

"Isles" or "isles of the sea" was a common expression used to indicate far-off lands whose localities and names were unknown to the prophet, but which would become important in days of prophetic fulfillment. The whole world is in view in this chapter, and the thing described has never happened. It will all come true in the days of Antichrist, and will be one of the signs which will identify him positively.

## EZEKIEL 27

1 The word of the Lord came again unto me, saying,

2 Now, thou son of man, take up a lamentation for Tyrus;

3 And say unto Tyrus, O thou that art situate at the entry of the sea, which art a merchant of the people for many isles, Thus saith the Lord God; O Tyrus, thou hast said, I am of perfect beauty.

4 Thy borders are in the midst of the seas, thy builders have perfected thy beauty.

5 They have made all thy ship boards of fir trees of Senir: they have taken cedars from Lebanon to make masts for thee.

6 Of the oaks of Bashan have they made thine oars; the company of the Ashurites have made thy benches of ivory, brought out of the isles of Chittim.

7 Fine linen with broidered work from Egypt was that which thou spreadest forth to be thy sail; blue and purple from the isles of Elishah was that which covered thee.

8 The inhabitants of Zidon and Arvad were thy mariners: thy wise men, O Tyrus, that were in thee, were thy pilots.

9 The ancients of Gebal and the wise men

thereof were in thee thy calkers: all the ships of the sea with their mariners were in thee to occupy thy merchandise.

10 They of Persia and of Lud and of Phut were in thine army, thy men of war: they hanged the shield and helmet in thee; they set forth thy comeliness.

11 The men of Arvad with thine army were upon thy walls round about, and the Gammadims were in thy towers: they hanged their shields upon thy walls round about: they have made thy beauty perfect.

12 Tarshish was thy merchant by reason of the multitude of all kind of riches; with silver, iron, tin, and lead, they traded in thy fairs.

13 Javan, Tubal, and Meshech, they were thy merchants: they traded the persons of men and vessels of brass in thy market.

14 They of the house of Togarmah traded in thy fairs with horses and horsemen and mules.

15 The men of Dedan were thy merchants; many isles were the merchandise of thine hand: they brought thee for a present horns of ivory and ebony.

16 Syria was thy merchant by reason of the multitude of the wares of thy making: they occupied in thy fairs with emeralds, purple, and broidered work, and fine linen, and coral, and agate.

17 Judah, and the land of Israel, they were thy merchants: they traded in thy market wheat of Minnith, and Pannag, and honey, and oil, and balm.

18 Damascus was thy merchant in the multitude of the wares of thy making, for the multitude of all riches; in the wine of Helbon, and white wool.

19 Dan also and Javan going to and fro occupied in thy fairs: bright iron, cassia, and calamus, were in thy market.

20 Dedan was thy merchant in precious clothes for chariots.

21 Arabia, and all the princes of Kedar, they occupied with thee in lambs, and rams, and goats: in these were they thy merchants.

22 The merchants of Sheba and Raamah, they were thy merchants: they occupied in thy fairs with chief of all spices, and with all precious stones, and gold.

23 Haran, and Canneh, and Eden, the merchants of Sheba, Asshur, and Chilmad, were thy merchants.

24 These were thy merchants in all sorts of things, in blue clothes, and broidered work, and in chests of rich apparel, bound with cords, and made of cedar, among thy merchandise.

25 The ships of Tarshish did sing of thee in thy market: and thou wast replenished, and made very glorious in the midst of the seas.

26 Thy rowers have brought thee into great waters: the east wind hath broken thee in the midst of the seas.

27 Thy riches, and thy fairs, thy merchandise, thy mariners, and thy pilots, thy calkers, and the occupiers of thy merchandise, and all thy men of war, that are in thee, and in all thy company which is in the midst of thee, shall fall into the midst of the seas in the day of thy ruin.

28 The suburbs shall shake at the sound of the cry of thy pilots.

29 And all that handle the oar, the mariners, and all the pilots of the sea, shall come down from their ships, they shall stand upon the land;

30 And shall cause their voice to be heard against thee, and shall cry bitterly, and shall cast up dust upon their heads, they shall wallow themselves in the ashes:

31 And they shall make themselves utterly bald for thee, and gird them with sackcloth, and they shall weep for thee with bitterness of heart and bitter wailing.

32 And in their wailing they shall take up a

lamentation for thee, and lament over thee, saying, What city is like Tyrus, like the destroyed
in the midst of the sea?

33  When thy wares went forth out of the seas,
thou filledst many people; thou didst enrich the
kings of the earth with the multitude of thy riches
and of thy merchandise.

34  In the time when thou shalt be broken by
the seas in the depths of the waters thy merchandise and all the company in the midst of thee
shall fall.

35  All the inhabitants of the isles shall be astonished at thee, and their kings shall be sore
afraid, they shall be troubled in their countenance.

36  The merchants among the people shall hiss
at thee; thou shalt be a terror, and never shalt
be any more.

This is an amazing description of a future city
when you consider that it was written 2,500 years
ago.

## The Prince of Tyrus

Ezekiel tells us about the prince of Tyrus and
the king of Tyrus, which would seem to suggest
that the city of Tyre is Antichrist's political capital
just as Babylon will be the religious and com-
mercial center of the world. In Ezekiel the prince
of Tyrus is not a type of Antichrist; he is Antichrist.
The king of Tyrus is not a type of Satan; he is
Satan, as will be evident when you read the text.

EZEKIEL 28

2  Son of man, say unto the prince of Tyrus,
Thus saith the Lord God; Because thine heart is
lifted up, and thou hast said, I am a God, I sit in
the seat of God, in the midst of the seas; yet thou
art a man, and not God, though thou set thine
heart as the heart of God.

Paul says that Antichrist will sit in the temple of God showing himself that he is God. This characteristic of Antichrist may not be fully developed at the start; some prophecies will take place after the Rapture.

Jesus refers to the abomination of desolation spoken of by Daniel. Daniel mentions this four times, but in no place does he tell what it means. There could be no abomination greater than this Man of Sin entering the temple and trying to be God. Although this may not happen until after the Rapture, Antichrist's attitude toward God may be visible from the start.

### EZEKIEL 28

3 Behold, thou art wiser than Daniel; there is no secret that they can hide from thee:

4 With thy wisdom and with thine understanding thou hast gotten thee riches, and hast gotten gold and silver into thy treasures:

5 By thy great wisdom and by thy traffick hast thou increased thy riches, and thine heart is lifted up because of thy riches:

Although the rise of Antichrist may be made possible because of a world economic crisis connected with wars and threats of wars, he will soon change all that and bring about the greatest world prosperity and tranquillity ever to be achieved. This is one of the reasons why it will be so difficult to identify him as Antichrist. Everybody loves Santa Claus. The end of this prosperity is recorded in Revelation, but in recording it John describes the extent of the abundance that Antichrist will bestow upon the world.

### REVELATION 18

9 And the kings of the earth, who have committed fornication and lived deliciously with her, shall bewail her, and lament for her, when they

shall see the smoke of her burning,

10 Standing afar off for the fear of her torment, saying, Alas, alas that great city Babylon, that mighty city! for in one hour is thy judgment come.

11 And the merchants of the earth shall weep and mourn over her; for no man buyeth their merchandise any more:

12 The merchandise of gold, and silver, and precious stones, and of pearls, and fine linen, and purple, and silk, and scarlet, and all thyine wood, and all manner vessels of ivory, and all manner vessels of most precious wood, and of brass, and iron, and marble,

13 And cinnamon, and odours, and ointments, and frankincense, and wine, and oil, and fine flour, and wheat, and beasts, and sheep, and horses, and chariots, and slaves, and souls of men.

Antichrist will raise the world from the depths of despondency to the heights of prosperity and glory. It is going to be difficult to oppose such a man and even to persuade people that he is Antichrist.

"With thy wisdom and with thine understanding thou hast gotten thee riches." Daniel says that he will understand dark sentences. His wisdom will be such that people will readily connect him with God in their thinking. Over and over again powerful men have so impressed the world that many people thought they were Antichrist, but there is coming a man with such wisdom and understanding that no one will think he is Antichrist except those who have understanding of the prophetic Scriptures.

When Satan takes over the body of Antichrist after the Rapture, there will be a dual personality. Antichrist will continue as a man until the end, and Satan will continue as Satan until the end. At the time of the coming of Christ Antichrist will meet an ignominious death.

## The King of Tyrus

Ezekiel 28:12-19 is one of the most difficult passages in the Bible, yet it is extremely important to the subject of Antichrist. Incarnation is a mystery that cannot be adequately explained in human words. Paul referred to the incarnation of Satan as the mystery of iniquity. Satan is the most powerful being in all creation. Revelation says that when he fell away from God, he carried with him one-third of the angels of heaven.

Satan was so great and so powerful that he thought he could defeat God and set himself up in place of God. He will attempt to prevent the resurrection. This attempt will bring about his ultimate defeat. He will be cast out of heaven and down to the earth, where he will take up his position in the body of a man, and we have the mystery of a satanic incarnation. Revelation says people will worship the dragon; they cannot see the dragon because he is a spirit. Antichrist will produce a great image or idol, and in worshipping the idol they will be worshipping Satan. When Jesus said, "I beheld Satan as lightning fall from heaven," He was speaking prophetically. It has not happened yet; it will happen at the Rapture.

Satan is going to be humiliated, dying like a man, while his spirit will be cast into the bottomless pit for 1,000 years. Isaiah tells the whole process as follows:

### ISAIAH 14

12 How art thou fallen from heaven, O Lucifer, son of the morning! how art thou cut down to the ground, which didst weaken the nations!

13 For thou hast said in thine heart, I will ascend into heaven, I will exalt my throne above the stars of God: I will sit also upon the mount of the congregation, in the sides of the north:

14 I will ascend above the heights of the clouds;
I will be like the most High.

15 Yet thou shalt be brought down to hell, to
the sides of the pit.

16 They that see thee shall narrowly look upon
thee, and consider thee, saying, Is this the man
that made the earth to tremble, that did shake
kingdoms?

In Ezekiel 28 the two persons are brought together, the prince of Tyrus and the king of Tyrus,
Antichrist and Satan. Although Satan does not actually reign on earth as a man until after the Rapture, the association between him and Antichrist
is very close, as we shall see when we consider
his rise to power. Make no mistake. Antichrist
and Satan will be as nearly one as Satan can con-
trive. There will be miracles, even at the start,
that will startle and deceive the whole world, except those who know what to expect, those that
have wisdom and understanding in the Scriptures.
As we approach the time of the rise of Antichrist,
this information will become extremely important
to all Christians.

Probably the greatest of all heresies, when you
consider all its consequences, is the false teaching
that none of these things can happen before the
Rapture. It throws Christians off their guard and
makes them wide open to Satan's masterpiece of
deceit.

### EZEKIEL 28

12 Son of man, take up a lamentation upon
the king of Tyrus, and say unto him, Thus saith
the Lord God; Thou sealest up the sum, full of
wisdom, and perfect in beauty.

The commentators find this a difficult verse
to translate. It seems to suggest that when God
made Satan, He went the limit beyond which He
could not go. God could not make an angel more

perfect than Satan without duplicating Himself.

### EZEKIEL 28

13 Thou hast been in Eden the garden of God; every precious stone was thy covering, the sardius, topaz, and the diamond, the beryl, the onyx, and the jasper, the sapphire, the emerald, and the carbuncle, and gold: the workmanship of thy tabrets and of thy pipes was prepared in thee in the day that thou wast created.

God came down into Eden and talked face to face with Adam and Eve. The only other spirit to visit Eden was Satan. This identifies him beyond any question. It would appear from Ezekiel that Satan had a dazzling beauty. It is no wonder that Eve was impressed. How could any being with such beauty and grandeur be bad?

### EZEKIEL 28

14 Thou art the anointed cherub that covereth; and I have set thee so: thou wast upon the holy mountain of God; thou hast walked up and down in the midst of the stones of fire.

The Jews anointed their kings. The word "Christ" means anointed. Satan was the anointed cherub. He was the king of all cherubim. He walked up and down in the midst of the stones of fire (the Milky Way?). It is impossible to contemplate the extent of Satan's power and authority. He could even challenge God with some apparent chance of success.

### EZEKIEL 28

15 Thou wast perfect in thy ways from the day that thou wast created, till iniquity was found in thee.

Here God reminds Satan that in spite of his power and magnificence, he is a created being. What caused Satan to fall? It may have been jealousy. Sometime back there in the distant past, God may have made an announcement that He was going to have a bride for Christ. Satan knew that God would not take a bride for His Son from a lower order of life. The announcement meant that God would have a people who would "shine as the brightness of the firmament" (Dan. 12:3; Matt. 13:43), who would surpass Satan with all his beauty and grandeur, and would become a part of the family of God. Satan must prevent this at all cost. What Satan did not know was that God could not produce that bride by creation, but He could do it by redemption, by death and resurrection. Christ is the firstfruits of the resurrection, and we will be like Christ, worthy to be presented as the daughter in the family of God. The Psalmist presents this scene.

### PSALM 45

9 Kings' daughters were among thy honourable women: upon thy right hand did stand the queen in gold of Ophir.

10 Hearken, O daughter, and consider, and incline thine ear; forget also thine own people, and thy father's house;

11 So shall the king greatly desire thy beauty: for he is thy Lord; and worship thou him.

12 And the daughter of Tyre shall be there with a gift; even the rich among the people shall intreat thy favour.

13 The king's daughter is all glorious within: her clothing is of wrought gold.

14 She shall be brought unto the king in raiment of needlework: the virgins her companions that follow her shall be brought unto thee.

15 With gladness and rejoicing shall they be brought: they shall enter into the king's palace.

16 Instead of thy fathers shall be thy children, whom thou mayest make princes in all the earth.

17 I will make thy name to be remembered in

all generations: therefore shall the people praise
thee for ever and ever.

### EZEKIEL 28

16 By the multitude of thy merchandise they
have filled the midst of thee with violence, and
thou hast sinned: therefore I will cast thee as pro-
fane out of the mountain of God: and I will destroy thee, O covering cherub, from the midst of
the stones of fire.

When we speak of the fall of Satan, we do not
mean his being cast out of heaven; we mean his
fall from the grace of God perhaps long before
God created the earth. Here we conjecture because God does not give the time. Satan appeared
before the throne of God and accused Job. Revelation says he will accuse the saints before the throne
of God day and night, but when he marshalls
all his forces, one-third of the angels of heaven
will join him in a final great effort to prevent
the Bride from taking her position with God. Revelation says, "There was war in heaven." This is
an all-out attempt on the part of Satan, and it
results in his first defeat where he loses ground.
Satan has suffered many a defeat in the past, but
he still remained in heaven. This time he will be
cast out of heaven and down to the earth. He will
make his last stand upon the earth.

### EZEKIEL 28

17 Thine heart was lifted up because of thy
beauty, thou hast corrupted thy wisdom by reason
of thy brightness: I will cast thee to the ground,
I will lay thee before kings, that they may behold
thee.
18 Thou hast defiled thy sanctuaries by the
multitude of thine iniquities, by the iniquity of thy
traffick; therefore will I bring forth a fire from
the midst of thee, it shall devour thee, and I will

bring thee to ashes upon the earth in the sight of
all them that behold thee.

19 All they that know thee among the people
shall be astonished at thee: thou shalt be a terror,
and never shalt thou be any more.

Satan does not become king of Tyrus till after
the Rapture so this is not to be considered in
reference to the identification of Antichrist. But
Antichrist will be completely inspired by Satan
from the start. Satan repeats his tactics. He appeared very attractive to Eve in the Garden. It
worked. Satan will try it again. In the Garden
Satan did not appear as Satan; he appeared as
a gorgeous serpent, very beautiful and attractive.
At the start Satan will not appear as Satan or
the king of Tyrus; he will appear as a man whom
the whole world can adore. He will capture the
imagination of many people so that the whole world
will be deceived. Preachers will extol his virtues
to the skies. It may be very unpopular to call
him Antichrist.

That is why God says in Revelation: "Here
is wisdom; let him who hath understanding count
the number of the beast." The world will not simply be subjected to deceit; it will be deceit on
a grand scale such as the world has never experienced. We cannot make this too emphatic.
Some of the most seemingly spiritual people will
be 100 percent deceived.

## CHAPTER 4

# Antichrist and the Nations

When we consider Antichrist and the nations, Antichrist and the saints, Antichrist and the Jews, Antichrist and Communism, there seems to be on the surface a lack of harmony. We might ask ourselves: How could all these situations exist at the same time? The method employed by many writers is to disregard the scriptures that seem to be out of harmony with their theories. There must be a better way. In this book I am not going to leave out any details simply because they are difficult to analyze. In some cases only the actual events will give us the solution to the problem. Circumstance will reveal it.

When we think of Antichrist and the nations, we think of Daniel because he was the prophet to the nations. He began with his own time when the Babylonian Empire was at its height. He predicted the fall of Babylon and the rise of the Medes and the Persians, usually known as the Persian Empire. He foresaw the dramatic fall of the Persian Empire and the rise of the Empire of Greece under the leadership of Alexander the Great. He saw the breaking up of Alexander's Empire into four parts.

He called all three of those empires by name.
The only one he did not name was the last one,
the Roman Empire. He told Nebuchadnezzar about
the rise of the fourth world empire and how it
would break up into many nations, and that these
nations would exist until the coming of Christ to
set up His Kingdom, which would be an everlasting
kingdom. Daniel predicted the dramatic rise of
a man who will hold sway over a large part of
the earth until he is defeated by the coming of
Christ. Daniel called this man the "little horn."

## The Little Horn

Daniel had four separate visions concerning
world empires. In three of them he used symbols.
In the first vision the symbols were the parts of
a great image. The head stood for the Babylonian
Empire, the arms might be labeled Persia and
Media; they came together in the chest to sym-
bolize the Empire of the Medes and Persians. The
trunk was brass which in Daniel's day would be
copper. The two legs were the two parts of the
Roman Empire, Europe and Asia. The ten toes
represented the dividing of the empire into many
countries, ten being a round number. Daniel predicted that Christ will come while these nations
of Europe still exist. No world catastrophe is going
to destroy these nations.

Daniel's second vision tells the same story of
the rise and fall of four world empires, except
that Daniel changed the symbols from the image
to wild beasts—a lion, a bear, a leopard, and an
unnamed beast. The beast had ten horns corre-
sponding to the ten toes of the image. The ten
horns represent the nations that were carved out
of the old Roman Empire. Again, ten is a round
number. The nations that were in the Roman Em-

pire are seldom exactly ten, but always approx-
imately ten. In the end they may be exactly ten.
Boundary lines have changed somewhat during
the years, and are still subject to change.

Daniel said, "I considered the horns." Possibly
the reason that Daniel changed his symbols from
those of the image to the four wild beasts is that
Daniel wanted to put action into the symbols. When
Daniel considered the horns, he was watching for
action. While the horns remained motionless like
the ten toes, no specific prophecy was being fulfilled beyond the fact of their existence.

Daniel was watching for action; that is the
exact situation we find ourselves in now. The nations are there; that fact alone is a prophetic fulfillment, but nothing of a prophetic nature has
happened among them. The final beast, the Roman
Empire, has been prophetically in a state of sus-
pended animation for a period of about 1500 years.
While this situation remains there will be little
prophetic fulfillment, but when the action foretold
by Daniel starts, there will be plenty of excitement.

It has been almost universally taught that the
ten horns which come out of the head of the beast,
represent the nations of Europe coming together
to form one empire which is the revival of the
Roman Empire. That is not exactly what Daniel
said. The ten horns of the beast correspond exactly to the ten toes of the image. Daniel said that
the ten toes mean, to use Daniel's words, "the
kingdom shall be divided."

The ten toes and the ten horns therefore represent not a revival of the Roman Empire, but the
breaking up of the old Roman Empire into many
countries. The revival of the Roman Empire might
be argued from other prophecies, but not from
this particular prophecy. The teaching has been
that the nations that come out of the Roman Em-

pire will unite and appoint a head, and that that
head is Antichrist. The prophecy is actually the
reverse of that. The man comes first, and he forms
the empire. We do not look for a revival of the
Roman Empire first, but first there will come a
man who will dominate the nations, partly by force
and partly by political action.

Everything previous to the rise of the little horn
has been fulfilled. The great empires of Babylon,
Persia, Greece, and Rome have come and gone
just as Daniel predicted. Now we come to the next
step, the rise of the little horn.

### DANIEL 7

8 I considered the horns, and, behold, there
came up among them another little horn, before
whom there were three of the first horns plucked
up by the roots: and, behold, in this horn were eyes
like the eyes of man, and a mouth speaking great
things.

Daniel had no map of Europe nor any conception of how Europe would look 2,500 years hence.
If Daniel had had a map, he would not have needed
the symbol. We follow Daniel's example when we
consider and study a map of the nations that were
symbolized by the horns. These are the nations
of southern Europe. A line would be drawn across
Germany—almost exactly the line which separates
East Germany from West Germany today. The
line would run along the southern border of Czech-
oslovakia. The Roman Empire took in Hungary,
Bulgaria, and Romania as well as Turkey. Even
the northern border of the Black Sea could be considered a part of the old Roman Empire. It took
in Syria, Palestine, and Egypt, including the southern coast of the Mediterranean Sea.

Daniel was not interested in any movement
among the horns that left them intact—as all wars
to date have done. War after war has raged across

Europe, but after each was over, the nations were still there. The horns were intact. A few border-lines may have changed, but the nations were still substantially the same. Wars such as World War I and World War II have been unimportant as far as prophecy is concerned. They were not noted by Daniel.

*"And, behold, there came up among them an-other little horn."* This is the beginning of the end. There is no prophecy in Daniel after the little horn, except a notation of the fact that after the little horn is disposed of, the saints will possess the Kingdom. Therefore, all prophecies about Anti-christ in the Bible, which are many, must apply to this one man. When this man arrives, all proph-ecies concerning things prior to the Second Com-ing of Christ must be fulfilled in his lifetime. Al-though prophecy sometimes seems to be slow in developing because the time is not ripe, there will be what amounts to an avalanche of prophetic fulfillment after this man arrives on the scene. These prophecies involve not only the nations, but the church, the Jews, and all society. Many of them will be happening at the same time. It will be hard to keep up with them.(See map, page 154.)

This man has been called the little horn. Later on, Daniel notes that he was more stout than his fellows. He starts weak and becomes strong. This man is to be Antichrist because he is the one that is cast into the lake of fire at the coming of Christ. His destruction marks the climax of Daniel's prophecies.

### DANIEL 7

21 I beheld, and the same horn made war with the saints, and prevailed against them;

22 Until the Ancient of days came, and judg-ment was given to the saints of the most High; and the time came that the saints possessed the king-dom.

It should be noted that the symbol "little horn" applies equally well to the nation and to the man. This is true in both Daniel and Revelation. In a dictatorship it is not necessary to distinguish between the dictator and the nation. We often speak of the man at the head of the nation when we imply that we are thinking of what the nation is doing.

Daniel used the symbols of gold and silver in the same way. He said to Nebuchadnezzar, "Thou art this head of gold. And after thee shall arise another kingdom inferior to thee."

In the prophetic Scriptures we sometimes encounter the neuter gender first, "It had ten horns." That is, the empire was made up of about ten nations. Then later a change is made to the masculine gender. Daniel said that he "beheld till the beast was slain and his body destroyed." The point is this: There will be a nation of no great significance at the start. A man will become the head of this nation. Then the man will grow in importance until he becomes greater than the nation. From this point on, the nation is more or less forgotten and the man becomes a world figure.

That which Daniel saw was not the immediate revival of the Roman Empire, but the arrival of a man. If there is any revival of the Roman Empire, it will be the work of this man. It is not the empire that produces the man, but the man who constructs the empire.

This man is the most sensational figure in prophecy. He dominates the prophecies concerning the Jews, the nations, and the church. To trace his character and his actions would take us into many parts of the Bible. Some things said about him are so unbelievable that they have seldom been taken at face value. God himself notes this fact. He said through the prophet Habakkuk: "I

will work a work in your days, which ye will not
believe, though it be told you."

His rise will probably be the most spectacular
and world-shaking event that has ever happened.
All the world will wonder at him "whose coming
is after the working of Satan." Here is a man
who completely represents Satan, just as the serpent did in the Garden of Eden, and who is just
as deceitful.

*"Behold, in this horn were eyes like the eyes
of man."* The first beast, the lion, was given a
man's heart. This little horn has a man's eyes.
The "man's heart" evidently refers to the excellent character of the king, demonstrated in his
public confession of God. Though this little horn
retains his beastly heart, yet he has the eyes of
a man. The eyes are a part of the symbol. (We
would expect a man to have eyes.) Usually, eyes
refer to intelligence, and that would probably be
the meaning of eyes in a symbol. This feature
is explained in the next vision: He will understand
dark sentences.

### DANIEL 8

23 And in the latter time of their kingdom,
when the transgressors are come to the full, a
king of fierce countenance, and understanding
dark sentences, shall stand up.

This is satanic intelligence. His coming is "after
the working of Satan" and his power will be due
to his super knowledge. This is no ordinary individual. Man's knowledge is reaching tremendous
heights and depths. Today this knowledge is being
directed toward implements of destruction. So
great has been the progress (?) that no one in
the world is safe. Man, and hence Satan, can now
actually wipe life off the face of the earth. If
this is not the end of the age, how can we go

beyond it? We have reached the ultimate.

The world is coming right up to the brink of disaster. It is Satan's big chance. He will rule the world if he can, destroy it if he must. Antichrist will "save" the world. He is "the" man of his day. He will know something beyond what the scientists know. He is able to make war successfully, suddenly, dramatically, almost single-handedly, against the best that science can produce. Scientists will produce the ultimate weapon and Antichrist will go them one better.

REVELATION 13
4 And they worshipped the beast, saying, . . .
who is able to make war with him?

HABAKKUK 1
8 Their [his] horsemen shall come from far;
they shall fly.

Again let me illustrate. (Please bear in mind that this is an illustration; it is not given as a fulfillment.) Pierre Van Paassen, author of *The Forgotten Ally*, wrote: "I had just talked with Adolph Hitler in Bonn after one of his propaganda meetings. He upbraided me violently for daring to defend the Jews in his presence. 'You, who are an Aryan, a Nordic, a Teuton from the shores of the German OCEAN!' he screamed, 'why do you not see the menace of the Jews to our western civilization?' In his eyes I had seen the strange, unearthly fire of hatred and was convinced that the man would before long be the master of Germany. . . . Not a Jew will be seen in the Reich in ten years. Even Jewish names on the tombstones will be obliterated. . . . I say so because I have looked in the eyes of Adolph Hitler."

Although the eyes are a part of the symbol and therefore do not necessarily refer to the eyes of the man himself, eyes do reflect the inner man.

His diabolical intelligence would be reflected in
the eyes, and so one of the outstanding features
of this man when he appears may be his eyes.
This is the more likely because of the next characteristic of the little horn.

*"And a mouth speaking great things."* He literally talks his way into power by flatteries, promises of peace and prosperity. Daniel develops this
in his next vision (ch. 8). This feature of the little
horn is also a feature of the man.

### DANIEL 7
11 I beheld then because of the voice of the
great words which the horn spake: I beheld even
till the beast was slain, and his body destroyed,
and given to the burning flame.

### REVELATION 13
5 And there was given unto him a mouth
speaking great things and blasphemies; and
power was given unto him to continue forty and
two months.
6 And he opened his mouth in blasphemy
against God, to blaspheme his name, and his tab-
ernacle, and them that dwell in heaven.

These two special features of the horn, "a
mouth speaking great things" and "eyes like the
eyes of a man," are also the outstanding features
of the man. When he comes you will probably hear
a lot of talk about his eyes, and he will "do things"
to people. These two features are the identifying
marks by which you may know him, although there
will be no mistaking him because the prophecies
are so specific. This man is a "natural." He perfectly fits the times. He is just what the nations
want—a man who can free the world from fear—
terrible fear of impending destruction—and bring
to the nations wealth—amazing wealth. The world
has never seen or dreamed of the kind of wealth
this man will be able to produce.

The potential is being built up now. It is forming in so many places with such fantastic new discoveries and inventions that we simply cannot keep up with them. The General Electric Company once said that it was going to produce more in the next ten years than ever before. This is largely because of the marvelous new things it sees on the horizon.

All that the world needs today is a man capable of enforcing peace, along with a free transfer of goods to the world's markets. Then in a few years this world could be transformed into a paradise. This peace and security will be Satan's great false millennium by which he will deceive the whole world. Paul says:

I THESSALONIANS 5
3  When they shall say, Peace and safety; then sudden destruction cometh upon them. . . .

This is such an important subject of prophecy that a whole chapter of Revelation is given over entirely to it (ch. 18). With such a program as this to offer the world, it will not be necessary for the little horn to do much conquering by military force.

DANIEL 8
25  Through his policy also he shall cause craft to prosper in his hand. . . .

How can such a vast empire be acquired by pulling up by the roots only three horns? The fact is that this man will not actually acquire the empire by conquest, but rather by what comes out of his mouth. It is evident that most of the countries involved will be almost automatically on the side of the little horn, as a result of a powerful common enemy that had been on the point of destroying them. But there may be some captive countries that would not have a free choice until they were conquered. It would be necessary to pull up these horns by the roots. At the time of the rise of Antichrist there will be three countries that for some reason cannot be classed with the others. These may be countries of the Roman Empire occupied by some foreign power.

There are three such countries today: Hungary, Romania, Bulgaria. They were in the Roman Empire, but they are behind the Iron Curtain now. There are only three such countries. They may or may not be the ones that are involved in the rise of Antichrist. Antichrist will start with the Roman Empire, but his empire will eventually include all the four world empires of history.

Nebuchadnezzar's image as explained by Daniel depicted the rise and fall of the four world empires of history. The empires came and went exactly as the image pictured. Most of the history of the world which the image represented is past. The only item left is the disposition of the ten toes. A stone was cut out of the mountain without hands, and it struck the image on its toes, but not just the toes were destroyed; the entire image crumbled, and the wind blew it away. The whole image was standing when the stone struck it. Daniel is very specific about this. He mentions it twice—the gold, the silver, the brass, the iron, and the clay all crumbled when the stone struck the toes.

Nebuchadnezzar's image must stand again. The empire of Antichrist will eventually reach out and take in all the lands occupied by the four world empires. This extends even into India and takes in most of the Middle East.

Revelation also suggests this same thing when it mentions the animals—the lion, the bear, the leopard, and the beast—which Daniel uses in his second vision to take in these same four empires.

Prophecy does not state how long it will take Antichrist to conquer this much territory. After the Rapture there will be wars and rebellions and revolutions throughout the world. After the Rapture there will be no peace, but before the Rapture, as we have already noted, there will probably be a profound peace and a worldwide prosperity.

There are many prophecies concerning Antichrist that will not be fulfilled until after the Rapture: such things as his persecution of the tribulation saints, his making the image speak, his attempt to force all people to receive his mark, and a series of campaigns described in Daniel 11. Inasmuch as these come after the Rapture, they are not factors in how to recognize Antichrist. We are concerned in this book only with those characteristics and events that will tend to identify him when he first arrives on the scene. There could be quite a number of years between the rise of Antichrist and the Rapture. (See map, page 155.)

## Daniel 8

Daniel had a third vision of the rise of Antichrist in which he used symbols. That is found in the eighth chapter of Daniel, but that chapter is so involved in controversy that we will take it up verse by verse.

### Vision of the Ram and the He-Goat

The Babylonian Empire—Its End

DANIEL 8

1 In the third year of the reign of king Belshazzar a vision appeared unto me, even unto

me Daniel, after that which appeared unto me
at the first.

At the time of this chapter, we are nearing
the end of the Babylonian Empire. Its last reigning
monarch was Belshazzar, in whose short reign
Babylon, the head of gold, was to be weighed and
found wanting. In the language of chapter 7, the
lion (Babylon) is about to give place to the bear
(Persia).

The visions of Daniel concern the future, not
the past; therefore, after the Babylonian Empire
had actually passed into history, Daniel began his
new prophecy with the new empire, Persia. As
always, the purpose of this new vision (ch. 8) is
to add details not found in the earlier ones (chs.
2 and 7).

Concerning the new symbols of chapter 8, it
is well to remember that all symbols and parables
follow a pattern. They are never strained to cover
more ground than they are naturally capable of
doing. Instead, a new parable or symbol is employed. This principle is well illustrated in the New
Testament in the parables of the kingdom, where
there is a separate parable for each separate truth.
The same kingdom is likened to seed, to buried
treasure, to a pearl, or to fish in a net. These
widely different symbols are used to illustrate different phases of the same thing. Symbols are limited in their application and must not be carried
beyond their natural function; instead, new symbols are employed to express new features.

This is also Daniel's method. In chapter 8 the
bear of the previous vision becomes a ram; the
leopard, a goat. The beast of chapter 7 does not
appear except in its final form. The first vision
(ch. 2) emphasized Babylon and the Kingdom of
Heaven; the second vision (ch. 7) passed over

Babylon and Persia and Greece with one verse each, but specialized on the fourth empire—the Roman Empire. The third vision (ch. 8) fills in details about the Persian and the Grecian empires, but, note carefully, it skips entirely the Roman Empire, except for the little horn. Each symbol is not strained to cover any more than it can do naturally. All the visions culminate with either the establishing of the Kingdom or the destruction of Antichrist (which is actually the same thing).

Although symbols are changed in order to bring into view new features and events, there is always enough similarity so that they can be easily identified. For instance, the numerical note of the second world empire is the figure two. (The image had two arms; the bear, two sides; and the ram, two horns.) The numerical note of the third empire is the figure four. (The leopard had four wings; the goat grew four horns.) Then, too, the fourth empire had iron legs and iron teeth. The emergence of the final Antichrist is symbolized by a "little horn."

## The Ram—The Persian Empire

### DANIEL 8

2 And I saw in a vision; and it came to pass, when I saw, that I was at Shushan in the palace, which is in the province of Elam; and I saw in a vision, and I was by the river of Ulai.

3 Then I lifted up mine eyes, and saw, and, behold, there stood before the river a ram which had two horns: and the two horns were high; but one was higher than the other, and the higher came up last.

The province of Elam, where Daniel was when he saw the vision, was east of the city of Babylon across the Euphrates and Tigris rivers. The ram corresponds to the bear that got up, first on one side and then on the other (ch. 7). The Persian

Empire, which was to conquer Babylon, was made up of two countries: Media, with its ancient people, and Persia, with its more modern tribe. Therefore it was called the Medo-Persian Empire.

Symbols are always explained by some means. For instance, the first of the four parts of the image was explained to Nebuchadnezzar by Daniel: "Thou art this head of gold." Again we have in chapter 8 a positive statement as to the identity of the second kingdom "The ram which thou sawest having two horns are the kings of Media and Persia" (Dan. 8:20). "King" is often used in place of kingdom, and so the symbol may be applied either to the king, or to the kingdom, or to both. In Daniel 2:39 Nebuchadnezzar is told, "After thee shall arise another kingdom inferior to thee."

## Expansion Northwest
### DANIEL 8
4 I saw the ram pushing westward, and northward, and southward; so that no beasts might stand before him, neither was there any that could deliver out of his hand; but he did according to his will, and became great.

The expansion of empire in those days was always toward the west, north, and to some extent, south. This general direction of conquest continued until all southern Europe was included, right to the Atlantic Ocean. This is an interesting note, inasmuch as in the last days the direction of movement will be in the reverse until Babylon, Persia, and Elam are again segments of a world empire.

## The Goat—The Grecian Empire
### DANIEL 8
5 And as I was considering, behold, an he goat came from the west on the face of the whole

earth, and touched not the ground: and the goat had a notable horn between his eyes.

6 And he came to the ram that had two horns, which I had seen standing before the river, and ran unto him in the fury of his power.

7 And I saw him come close unto the ram, and he was moved with choler against him, and smote the ram, and brake his two horns: and there was no power in the ram to stand before him, but he cast him down to the ground, and stamped upon him: and there was none that could deliver the ram out of his hand.

8 Therefore the he goat waxed very great: and when he was strong, the great horn was broken; and for it came up four notable ones toward the four winds of heaven.

Here the numerical notes that connect with the other visions are the figures one and four. One connects with the image—the trunk of the image was one as contrasted with the arms, legs, and toes. Four connects with the four wings and four heads of the leopard.

Again we have the inspired interpretation of the details. "And the rough goat is the king of Grecia: and the great horn that is between his eyes is the first king" (Dan. 8:21). The "first king" of Greece was Alexander the Great. He made swift conquest of the world, defeated the Persians, and became a world ruler. However, when the empire of Alexander reached its greatest extent, the young conqueror fell victim of his own excesses and died. At his death there was great confusion, and a number of men who tried to take over the empire were slain. Finally, the empire was divided into four parts ("four notable ones"), each with a separate ruler. They were: (1) Macedonia and Greece, (2) Asia Minor, (3) Syria, Babylonia, Media, etc., (4) Egypt, Cyprus, etc.

## Its Little Horn—Antichrist

### DANIEL 8

9 And out of one of them came forth a little horn, which waxed exceeding great, toward the south, and toward the east, and toward the pleasant land.

Up to this point the commentators are pretty much in agreement; but from this point on, difficulties multiply. Therefore it will be necessary to stick closely to the rules of interpretation and let the scriptures interpret themselves. There are many textual difficulties, but the modern versions agree substantially with the Authorized Version. In place of pleasant land, we read "beauteous land," or "glorious land"; but in any case the reference would have to be to Palestine.

The interpretation revolves around the identity of "the little horn." With one accord the commentators say the little horn is Antiochus Epiphanes. It is true he persecuted the Jews in Palestine but not to the extent of Hitler's persecution. Antiochus did not fulfill the prophecy, or any part of it. It is said that he put a sow in the temple and caused the Jews to worship it. This is said to be "the transgression of desolation" mentioned in the thirteenth verse.

Daniel mentions "the abomination of desolation" a number of times (9:27; 11:31; 12:11), always in reference to Antichrist. In the Olivet Discourse (Matt. 24) Jesus said, "When ye therefore shall see the abomination of desolation, spoken of by Daniel, the prophet, standing in the holy place. . . . " Then Jesus goes on to tell about the signs of His coming again. Here Jesus referred to this "abomination of desolation" as something future, not past. He connected it with the perse-

cution of the Jews by Antichrist, not Antiochus.
Antiochus does not appear in prophecy. His acts
had no prophetic significance and no lasting results. In importance he does not approach Adolph
Hitler, whose persecutions do have prophetic significance and lasting results—he forced the Jews
to return to Palestine—and so for the first time
since Daniel, we have an independent Jewish state.

Although in the different visions the symbols
may differ, there are always points of contact and
of similarity, so that the various parts may be
readily identified. This is done by the use of numbers and descriptive words. If, then, we find in
two successive visions such a highly descriptive
term as "little horn," it would have to refer to
the same thing in both places, or we have no basis
for interpretation.

You will notice that the little horn of Daniel
8 appears in the same relative position as the little
horn of Daniel 7, not only in reference to the other
visions of Daniel, but also in Revelation and the
Olivet Discourse. The stone was cut out "without
hand." All of the visions end with the destruction
of Antichrist. This little horn follows this pattern
exactly.

We also have an inspired explanation of the
vision of chapter 8. An angel appeared on purpose
to explain the meaning to Daniel and said, "Gabriel, make this man to understand the vision.
So he came near where I stood: . . . he said unto
me, Understand, O son of man" (vv. 16, 17). So
we follow here the explanation of the angel rather
than that of the commentaries. When the angel
says, "He shall also stand up against the Prince
of princes; but he shall be broken without hand,"
the angel is talking about the little horn. This statement could not be said of anybody else. Moreover,

it follows the pattern of all the visions. It is not consistent or even reasonable to make the symbol, "the little horn," apply to Antiochus and the explanation of the symbol to Antichrist. If Antiochus did not fulfill the symbol and in no way connects with the explanation of the symbol, he should be completely excluded from our thinking.

Chapter 8 skips from the third empire to the focal point of all the visions—the rise of Antichrist. (Details of the fourth empire, however, are found in the previous vision—chapter 7.) Note carefully that these visions cover 2,500 years of time. Many years have to be passed over with only a passing remark. The phrase in chapter 8 that carries us across the more than 2,000 years is this: "In the latter time of their kingdom" (v. 23).

The little horn, we are told, is to come out of one of the four winds of heaven (v. 8). Which wind it is, is immediately indicated: he will wax great toward the south, east, and toward Palestine. To do this, he will have to start in the north and west. The previous vision says that the little horn will conquer three countries of the Roman Empire. In the next vision, Daniel mentions the restoration of the kingdom, referring to the Roman Empire. In Revelation, the beast has ten horns, indicating again the Roman Empire.

### Geopolitics

In the first vision (ch. 2) the ten horns appeared as ten toes, ten nations that came out of the Roman Empire, and of them Daniel said, "In the days of these kings shall the God of heaven set up a kingdom" (2:44). The nucleus of Antichrist's kingdom will be the Roman Empire. To obtain this kingdom, he must wax great in three directions: south, east, and toward Palestine.

"The share of the earth controlled by each nation is a matter involving geography as well as government." In modern times, this principle has been developed into a science called geopolitics, which "is concerned with the dependence of the domestic and foreign politics of a people upon physical environment." Geopolitics was known in Germany by the Kaiser, and he based his hopes of world domination on it. But not until the end of World War I was the theory of geopolitics developed into a science and put into print. It then became the first principle of all would-be world conquerors.

Geopolitics has three basic principles: (1) Who rules East Europe commands the Heartland (the Middle East). (2) Who rules the Heartland commands the World-Island (Palestine). (3) Who rules the World-Island commands the world. Thus, he who rules East Europe commands the Middle East, commands Palestine, commands the world. (See the *Encyclopaedia Britannica* 1961 under Geopolitics and Sir Halford Mackinder.) In 1919 Sir Halford Mackinder wrote:

> A monkish map contemporary with the Crusades still hangs in Herford Cathedral. On it Jerusalem is marked as at the geographical center, the navel of the world; and on the floor of the Church of the Holy Sepulchre at Jerusalem they will show to this day the precise spot which is the center.
>
> If our study of the geographical realities as we now know them in their completeness is leading us to right conclusions, the medieval ecclesiastics were not far wrong.
>
> If the World-Island be inevitably the principal seat of humanity on this globe, and if Arabia, as the passage-land from Europe to the Indies and from the northern to the southern Heartland, be central in the World-Island, then the hill citadel

of Jerusalem has a strategic position with reference to world realities not differing essentially from its ideal position in the perspective of the Middle Ages.

Sir Halford saw the United States, Britain, Japan and other great nations as mere satellites of the dictator who held control of the World-Island. Palestine has always been a World-Island, and will be until the "law shall go forth out of Zion, and the word of the Lord from Jerusalem." The prophets knew about the World-Island. Now that all world action is centering in those lands, a great mass of prophecy is on the verge of fulfillment.

Acting on this theory, Russia captured and still holds three countries of Eastern Europe. Before and during the reign of Antichrist, the Middle East (the Heartland) will be the scene of the most violent activity. The final world battle, called Armageddon, is an attempt on the part of all nations to get control of Palestine or to prevent Christ and the saints from taking over that land.

Palestine always has been an island surrounded by enemies. It is becoming a World-Island. All conquerors recognize it as such. This fact was well known to the prophets. "Who commands the World-Island rules the world," says the author of geopolitics. Isaiah said the same thing:

### ISAIAH 2

2 And it shall come to pass in the last days, that the mountain of the Lord's house shall be established in the top of the mountains, and shall be exalted above the hills; and all nations shall flow unto it.

3 And many people shall go and say, Come ye, and let us go up to the mountain of the Lord, to the house of the God of Jacob; and he will teach us of his ways, and we will walk in his paths: for out of Zion shall go forth the law, and the word of the Lord from Jerusalem.

Antichrist will follow the same course. He will move toward the east and toward Palestine. He will take Eastern Europe. If Russia still holds it, he will defeat Russia. From the very beginning he will aim at Palestine. He will not make military conquest of Palestine until the time of Armageddon and then it will be too late.

Next in chapter 8:10-14 we have a scene that has been called the most difficult passage in prophecy. It would be if you were thinking about Antiochus Epiphanes. However, the prophet is talking about something vastly different from anything that happened historically between the time of the Old and New Testaments. This passage may be difficult, but it is extremely important. It contains the one element of mystery that makes the rise of Antichrist so much different from that of any conqueror that has preceded him.

The details of Antichrist's rise are unbelievable before they happen because Antichrist has his roots in outer space. God expressed this truth to Habakkuk:

### HABAKKUK 1
5 Behold ye among the heathen [nations], and regard, and wonder marvellously: for I will work a work in your days, which ye will not believe, though it be told you.

### *Satan Takes Over*

### DANIEL 8
10 And it waxed great, even to the host of heaven; and it cast down some of the host and of the stars to the ground, and stamped upon them.

11 Yea, he magnified himself even to the prince of the host, and by him the daily sacrifice was taken away, and the place of his sanctuary was cast down.

12 And an host was given him against the daily sacrifice by reason of transgression, and it cast down the truth to the ground; and it practised, and prospered.

13 Then I heard one saint speaking, and another saint said unto that certain saint which spake, How long shall be the vision concerning the daily sacrifice, and the transgression of desolation, to give both the sanctuary and the host to be trodden under foot?

14 And he said unto me, Unto two thousand and three hundred days; then shall the sanctuary be cleansed.

*"He magnified himself even to the prince of the host."* This section has been very difficult to translate; the versions all differ. The Authorized Version is as good as any, but one change should be noted. The *Pulpit Commentary* says of verse 11: "It is assumed that the little horn is the subject of this sentence; but horn is feminine in Hebrew, and the verbs here (in verse eleven) are in the masculine; this is against its being the nominative. The prince of the host, then must be the nominative of the verbs and subject of the sentence. The rendering of the first clause ought to be: 'Until the prince of the host magnify himself, and by himself he shall offer the daily sacrifice.' " Another rendering is: "Until the prince of the host shall make himself greater [than the little horn] and shall offer the daily sacrifice." This makes it much easier to understand.

The prince of the host is Satan. Revelation tells of his angels falling from heaven. Satan's great ambition is to be like God—not in perfection, but in power and glory. This was the first cause of his downfall.

ISAIAH 14
12 How art thou fallen from heaven, O Lucifer, son of the morning! how art thou cut down

to the ground, which didst weaken the nations!

13 For thou hast said in thine heart, I will ascend into heaven, I will exalt my throne above the stars of God: I will sit also upon the mount of the congregation, in the sides of the north:

14 I will ascend above the heights of the clouds; I will be like the most High.

15 Yet thou shalt be brought down to hell, to the sides of the pit.

16 They that see thee shall narrowly look upon thee, and consider thee, saying, Is this the man that made the earth to tremble, that did shake kingdoms;

17 That made the world as a wilderness, and destroyed the cities thereof; that opened not the house of his prisoners?

At the time of the end Satan will satisfy this consuming desire; he will sit in the temple of God showing himself that he is God (II Thess. 2:4). The abomination of desolation is Satan in the temple mockingly offering the daily sacrifice.

*"And it waxed great, even to the host of heaven; and it cast down some of the host and of the stars to the ground."* The host of heaven are the angels of heaven. Some are called fallen angels because they seem to have participated in the fall of Satan; they are Satan's angels. Sometimes people are surprised to find that these fallen angels are still in heaven. The fall has to do with their moral state, not their place of abode. When the sons of God came to present themselves before the Lord, Satan also came among them.

### JOB 1

6 Now there was a day when the sons of God came to present themselves before the Lord, and Satan came also among them.

Heaven is a big place; in fact, it may cover all outer space. It is quite certain that the space in the vicinity of the earth is infested by Satan's angels as well as demons of various orders. Prophecy is specific about the fact that the heavens as well as the earth must be cleansed. Both Isaiah and Revelation speak of the new heaven and the new earth.

### ISAIAH 65

17 For, behold, I create new heavens and a new earth: and the former shall not be remembered, nor come into mind.

### REVELATION 21

1 And I saw a new heaven and a new earth: for the first heaven and the first earth were passed away; and there was no more sea.

This cleansing starts in the heavens but is soon transferred to the earth.

Antichrist, whose coming is after the working of Satan, makes contact with the host of heaven. That is when Satan, using the physical properties of Antichrist, becomes a man.

There is no question that Revelation 12 has reference to the same event as Daniel 8:10:

### REVELATION 12

4 His tail drew the third part of the stars of heaven, and did cast them to the earth. . . .

9 And the great dragon was cast out, that old serpent, called the Devil, and Satan, which deceiveth the whole world: he was cast out into the earth, and his angels were cast out with him.

Satan will reign in person on the earth. The little horn will become Satan. How this is accomplished is told in Revelation 13.

Some of the wording here is difficult to translate because it deals with something beyond our comprehension. There are no words for it. This passage, however, is the key to the last days of the age. Scientists may discover the physical characteristics of outer space, but the earth will suddenly come to realize that the heavens are full of living beings who have designs on the earth.

Man is making conquest of outer space, but in so doing, he may be stirring up a nest of hornets. The most devastating realization which the people of the earth will ever experience will come when they suddenly wake up to the fact that instead of our making conquest of outer space, the beings of outer space are making conquest of the earth. This begins at the temple. Satan, as usual, is following God's pattern, for Jesus started at the temple. After the triumphal entry into Jerusalem, He went immediately to the temple and cleansed it. His coming again will be to the temple first, as far as the Jews are concerned.

### MALACHI 3
1  The Lord, whom ye seek, shall suddenly come to his temple.

Daniel deals with the coming of Satan as it relates to the nations. Revelation is concerned only with his relationship to the saints.

### 2300 Days

*"How long shall be the vision concerning the daily sacrifice, and the transgression of desolation, to give both the sanctuary and the host to be trodden under foot? And he said unto me, Unto 2300 days; then shall the sanctuary be cleansed."* These 2,300 days would amount to about 6 1/2 years. There is a 10-1/2-year period between the Rapture and the return of Christ. The last 7 years correspond to Daniel's 70th week. During the first 3 1/2 years of the 10-1/2-year period, Antichrist is engaged in getting rid of the saints. Then he turns his attention to the Jews. We do not know exactly when

these 2,300 days start, or where they end. We are informed here only of the total length of time in which the temple will be subject to desecration.

## An Inspired Explanation

### The Time of the End

#### DANIEL 8

15  And it came to pass, when I, even I Daniel, had seen the vision, and sought for the meaning, then, behold, there stood before me as the appearance of a man.

16  And I heard a man's voice between the banks of Ulai, which called, and said, Gabriel, make this man to understand the vision.

17  So he came near where I stood: and when he came, I was afraid, and fell upon my face: but he said unto me, Understand, O son of man: for at the time of the end shall be the vision.

18  Now as he was speaking with me, I was in a deep sleep on my face toward the ground: but he touched me, and set me upright.

19  And he said, Behold, I will make thee know what shall be in the last end of the indignation: for at the time appointed the end shall be.

"The time of the end," like "the day of the Lord" or "that day," is a reference to the events that lead up to the coming of Christ. This "time" is the focal point of all prophecy. Now and then a prophet gets a glimpse beyond the time of the end and sees something of the new beginning. This is particularly true of Isaiah, and of course of Revelation. But for the most part the prophets concentrated on the events leading up to the Second Coming of Christ and the establishing of the Kingdom of Heaven. That is the end of things as we know them today.

The dominant world figure at the time of the

end is Antichrist, called here "the little horn."
Three verses are given to the background, the empires of Persia and Greece.

### Persia and Greece

#### DANIEL 8

20 The ram which thou sawest having two horns are the kings of Media and Persia.

21 And the rough goat is the king of Grecia: and the great horn that is between his eyes is the first king.

22 Now that being broken, whereas four stood up for it, four kingdoms shall stand up out of the nation, but not in his power.

King Alexander died suddenly; no provision had been made for his successor. After much confusion, the empire was divided. None of Alexander's sons became a ruler, so his generals took over. Four kings stood up "but not in his power."

### Antichrist

#### DANIEL 8

23 And in the latter time of their kingdom, when the transgressors are come to the full, a king of fierce countenance, and understanding dark sentences, shall stand up.

24 And his power shall be mighty, but not by his own power: and he shall destroy wonderfully, and shall prosper, and practise, and shall destroy the mighty and the holy people.

Let us examine in greater detail these two verses phrase by phrase.

*"In the latter time of their kingdom."* Here we pass by all the years from Alexander to Antichrist and are brought to "the time of the end," as the angel said.

*"When the transgressors are come to the full."* Jesus referred to this particular evil time as "the harvest."

## MATTHEW 13

30 Let both grow together until the harvest: and in the time of harvest I will say to the reapers, Gather ye together first the tares, and bind them in bundles to burn them, but gather the wheat into my barn.

Harvest is the end of a growing season. The judgment day will be a harvest. God will judge only a finished work. He will allow evil to reach a harvest. "The time of trouble such as never was" will be due directly to the time of evil such as never was.

## DANIEL 12

1 And at that time shall Michael stand up, the great prince which standeth for the children of thy people: and there shall be a time of trouble, such as never was since there was a nation even to that same time: and at that time thy people shall be delivered, every one that shall be found written in the book.

But everything will be in its order. The reference to evil here is not to the moral condition of the people but to the spread of bad government. Those who are attempting to enslave the world and whose tactics are violence, lies, confiscation of property and rigged courts will reach the utmost limit of their potential. This is vividly expressed by Habakkuk, speaking on this same theme:

## HABAKKUK 1

2 O Lord, how long shall I cry, and thou wilt not hear! even cry out unto thee of violence, and thou wilt not save!

3 Why dost thou shew me iniquity, and cause me to behold grievance? for spoiling and violence are before me: and there are that raise up strife and contention.

4 Therefore the law is slacked, and judgment doth never go forth: for the wicked doth compass

about the righteous; therefore wrong judgment
proceedeth.

When this corruption has become so extensive
that the whole world is threatened, then the transgressors have "come to the full." It is to this situation that Jesus referred when He spoke of wars
and commotions, and added, "Be not terrified"—
indicating the threat not only to world peace but
to world safety. The transgressors will have terrifying weapons that will seemingly give them the
power to destroy all people.

*"A king of fierce countenance and understand-
ing dark sentences shall stand up."* This is the
angel's explanation of the "little horn." His coming is at a time of world crisis brought on by
"the transgressors" (8:23). They not only reach
their limits; they exceed their limits. Then something unexpected happens. What is said about Antichrist is not very extensive; but it does go a
long way toward filling in the other prophecies.
He is prominent in three relationships: to the
nations, to the Jews, and to the church. A harmony of all the references to him could reveal
a large amount of information. We have previously
noted Antichrist's eyes and mouth. Now we may
add "a fierce countenance." His appearance
should not be underrated, for it will have a lot
to do with his success—or, it may be more accurate
to say that the thing that makes him so powerful
also gives him his fierce look.

We may have to await the event to get the
full meaning of the phrase "understanding dark
sentences." The expression could mean that he
deals with familiar spirits or has some kind of
demon possession. Paul said his coming is after
the working of Satan. He will have a superior
knowledge supplied by Satan, which will give him
power to cope with every situation, even atomic
war.

*"His power shall be mighty, but not by his own power."* Again we are told that the rise of this man is going to be different from anything that has ever happened. That difference lies in the source of his power. It does not come from the science laboratories or from the research plants of industry. He will not have kept up with Russia in the development of atomic warfare, but he will have a certain knowledge that will make him master over anything the nations can produce.

Today, as never before, knowledge is power. Some nation could build up, by long scientific research, a vast system of nuclear warfare, even based in space, so that it could absolutely control every square mile of the earth; and one man, with a superior knowledge, could nullify the whole thing. Satan has that knowledge. Antichrist will not be impressed by the world's might. A man "whose coming is after the working of Satan" and who operates "not by his own power" will laugh at the world's armaments. Habakkuk puts it in these words:

HABAKKUK 1
    10 Yea, he scoffeth at kings, and princes are a derision unto him; he derideth every strong-hold; for he heapeth up dust and taketh it" (R.V.).

The more formidable the world's weapons, the more sensational will be Antichrist's exploits. They will bring him not only admiration and wonder but actual worship. His association with Satan will not embarrass him, although it will be well known, at least after the Rapture, for we are told:

REVELATION 13
    2 The dragon gave him his power, and his seat (throne), and great authority.
    4 And they worshipped the dragon which gave power unto the beast: and, they worshipped the

beast, saying, Who is like unto the beast? who
is able to make war with him?''

*"And he shall destroy wonderfully."* Young
translates this literally: "And wonderful things
he destroyeth." To get the full significance of this
remarkable prediction, you must recognize certain principles of interpretation. The prophets
never exaggerated; nearly all prophecy is under-
statement. The prophets dealt with extreme cases
where exaggeration would be impossible. To cross
the ocean the first time on a steamboat might
have seemed marvelous. Every great advance of
science has had its awesome aspects. Wonderful
things are commonplace today. But none are
wonderful enough to fulfill the prophecy, so that
we must yet have the most extraordinary things
that could possibly be realized. When the ultimate
comes, prophecy will be ready for fulfillment. We
may be justified in believing that we have reached
this place in prophetic development now when
nations have acquired the power to destroy the
earth and have begun the conquest of space.

The use of the word "destroy" is also signifi-
cant. The English word "destroy" is used to
translate a large number of Hebrew words with
various meanings. Here it means to destroy in
the literal sense of demolish so that the object
can no longer perform its intended function. How
up-to-date this sounds—"destroy wonderfully."
When the great nations are in a race to find the
most wonderful way of destroying, the nation that
can be the first to obtain the ultimate weapon will
rule the world. The race is on, but it will be
Antichrist, not Russia, who in the end will destroy wonderfully.

Whom will Antichrist destroy? This question
may be answered. He will not destroy his own
kingdom. Nor will he destroy the nations of the

Roman Empire; for concerning them Daniel said, "In the days of these kings shall the God of heaven set up a kingdom." Also, I do not believe he will destroy America. The Philadelphia and Laodicean and other churches are here, and the Laodicean Church at least is rich and increased with goods. Unless I am very misled, I believe the United States will almost have to be the principal location of the tribulation saints.

So far as I see, there is only one nation today that would stand in the way of Antichrist. Two conquerors, each with a consuming ambition to rule the world, could not long exist side by side. The only reason Russia has lasted as long as she has is that she has no competition—no other nation is threatening the whole world. When "the little horn stands up," everything will change. It will be either the one or the other. It is the little horn who destroys wonderfully.

*"He shall prosper and practise, and shall destroy the mighty and the holy people."* It now becomes necessary for us to orient ourselves by reference to the original vision (which is here being explained) and also by reference to other prophecies.

First, in reference to the vision:

### DANIEL 8
9 Out of one of them came forth a little horn, which waxed exceeding great, toward the south, and toward the east, and toward the pleasant land.

After Antichrist waxes great toward Palestine, there is a change which is brought about by the injection of spirit forces. Although from the start Satan will empower Antichrist, the actual presence of satanic beings on the earth will be something this world has not seen since the Flood. Then Antichrist will begin his war with the saints. We know from Revelation that this follows the Rapture immediately. In this connection we are told that he practiced and prospered (Dan. 8:12). The main feature of this phase of Antichrist's reign is the persecution of the tribulation saints. This puts the time of verses 10-12 in the middle of verse 24 (verse 24 being the explanation). That is the time when Satan begins to "practice" and to kill the saints. This harmonizes perfectly with Daniel 7 and also with the book of Revelation.

### Broken Without Hand

#### DANIEL 8

25 And through his policy also he shall cause craft to prosper in his hand; and he shall magnify himself in his heart, and by peace shall destroy many: he shall also stand up against the Prince of princes; but he shall be broken without hand.

*"By peace he (Antichrist) shall destroy many."* Two details need to be mentioned here. First, although the versions differ somewhat, they are quite generally agreed in translating "peace" by the word "treachery": "by treachery shall destroy many." The word also means "suddenly." (Daniel 11:21 supports the Authorized rendering "peace." Antichrist uses peace as an instrument of conquest. The modern term is cold war.) If we put this alongside of Daniel 7, we find that the little horn actually takes by force only three other nations of the Roman Empire. The rest of his empire he acquires by craft and treachery. This does not mean that Antichrist will not destroy other countries outside of the Roman Empire. They would not be included in this prophecy.

Second, "he stands up against the Prince of princes." He is anti-Christ. The statement here is brief because it is fully developed in parallel accounts.

## *True but Future*

### DANIEL 8

26 And the vision of the evening and the morning which was told is true: wherefore shut thou up the vision; for it shall be for many days.

27 And I Daniel fainted, and was sick certain days; afterward I rose up, and did the king's business; and I was astonished at the vision, but none understood it.

*"Shut thou up the vision."* It was the meaning of the prophecy, not the prophecy itself, that was shut up. The vision was made known, but none understood it. At the time, it had no particular function because its fulfillment was in the distant future. This illustrates one of the most important features of prophecy—its purpose. This is not an isolated case; it goes to the very heart of all prophecy.

Except for a few items which were fulfilled at the first advent of Christ and the beginning of the church, prophecy looks ahead to one period of time, not more than a generation long, in which will come the greatest changes of all time. The climax of all the ages is the Second Coming of Christ. It will outclass all the other world crises, such as the Flood, the Tower of Babel, the Exodus from Egypt, and even the miracles of Jesus. The Second Coming of Christ has a feature that was largely lacking in the previous crises—the active participation of the spirit world, or, as we call it, outer space.

*"I Daniel fainted and was sick."* It was not something Daniel ate that caused him to faint, but something he saw. Words in themselves are always inadequate to express a vision. We do not faint when we read what Daniel saw. In the same way, on the Mount of Transfiguration, though the disciples were completely overcome by what they

saw, merely reading about it in our day does not give us the same experience. But we may not have long to wait to see the fulfillment of Daniel's vision. If Daniel fainted because he saw a vision of a part of what is going to happen, what will be the experience of those who go through the actual events?

# CHAPTER 5

# World Conditions

The great men of history have been products of their times. If it had not been that the time of the Exodus was ripe, Moses might have remained an unknown figure tending the flocks of Jethro. Jesus liked to say, "Mine hour has not yet come." He became the Saviour of the world only when the time of the crucifixion had come.

Antichrist will be the product of his time. A figure so sensational could come only out of sensational times. A world crisis will produce Antichrist. Therefore, we may not look for him until his time has come. These world conditions are described both by Jesus and by the Old Testament prophet Habakkuk. The disciples asked Jesus, "What shall be the sign of thy coming, and the end of the age?" In His answer Jesus did not mention Antichrist by name, but almost everything He said connects with Antichrist in some other portion of Scripture.

The first thing Jesus mentioned was the rise of many false christs who would deceive many people, possibly many Christians. We have today a number of cults, some of them of long standing. These cults for the most part reflect the peculiarities of their founders. They all have enough truth to make them respectable and enough error to lead many people astray. Most of these cults have been with us too long to be involved in this prophecy. Jesus was talking about a very special situation, almost unbelievable, that will characterize the religious world at the time of the rise of Antichrist. Jesus' exact words are, "Take heed that no man deceive you, for many shall come in my name saying, I am Christ, and shall deceive many" (Matt. 24:4, 5). There is some question as to the proper translation of this verse. Mark and Luke in the Greek both leave out the word "Christ." The false christs say, "I am." They claim to be what Christ said He was, "the way, the truth, and the life."

These false christs are also a product of their times. In times of religious apathy there are few false christs; there is no lively interest in that direction. A host of false christs will appear only in a time of great religious fervor. They will be Satan's attempt to counteract a worldwide gospel effort.

Many teachers have been telling us that nothing prophetic can happen before the Rapture, that we have seen our last great revival. That is not true. A great many prophetic fulfillments must take place before the Rapture; prominent among them are a worldwide sweep of Christianity and an unveiling of the prophetic Scriptures. There is nothing in the world more powerful than a truth when its time has come. God told Daniel that his predictions would be sealed up (as far as their influence is concerned) until the time of the end; that is, until their time had come. Then many would run to and fro (preach and teach), and knowledge would be increased.

The Bible is full of truths that in the past have had little influence on the world. They have been for the most part disregarded by the church, but they are there for a purpose, and when their time has come, they will make a tremendous impact on the world. God has put in His Word a powerful punch for what the Bible calls "the time of the end." Satan will react by producing a host of false christs and false teachers. In Jesus' answer to the disciples, He puts this first, which might indicate that it is one of the first signs to look for.

## False Religions

Luke adds an important detail: *the time draweth near.* The deceivers will preach prophecy. There have always been deceivers preaching Christ and His coming again. There have always been wars and rumors of wars; these would not be signs unless there was something unusual about them, something that is different from anything that has happened before.

The unusual thing is that there will be *many* of them. False teachers and false religions will suddenly begin to multiply. They will pull so many people away from the church that the situation will really become serious.

There is a reason for this. The reason may be found in the clue *the time draweth near.* Satan reads the signs; he knows what to preach to get the people. The last days of this age will be tremendous. The world will be changing fast. Everybody will realize that Bible prophecy is being fulfilled. If under those circumstances the churches cannot supply the information so much in demand, others will.

Jesus knew this would happen and tried to correct it, but He is getting very little cooperation. The Olivet Discourse was not an accident. Jesus knew what He wanted to say to the Christians of this age, and He made a statement concerning the temple that would bring out the questions He wanted to answer. For nineteen hundred years Jesus' words have been disregarded. Until now, that has not been too serious because the message is for a certain time; but when that time comes, if the church then disregards it, false teachers will have a field day.

As Jesus sat there on the Mount and looked down through the years of time to the end of the gospel age, how wonderful it would have been if He could have said, "The churches will increase in knowledge of the Word until in the last days, when the world is plunged into its greatest crisis, the prophetic Word will be so well known that the churches can use it to spark a great worldwide revival, and there will be a great ingathering."

Instead, He had to warn Christians who would take heed not to be deceived by the many new teachers that would come preaching the truths that were designed for the church. The churches are not ready for what is coming on the world. They know a little area of truth which they repeat over and over again. There is a little circle of knowledge containing a few basic truths and a few Bible stories which are monotonously repeated year after year to the exclusion of all the rest of the Bible. It is the part of the Bible that has been left out of our thinking that is important today.

Possibly one-fourth of the Bible is prophecy. This is a large amount to leave out of our consideration, but when this part becomes vital because of world conditions, its omission creates a vacuum and false teachers rush in. The most troublesome and fastest-growing false religions make much of prophecy; in fact, that is their strength. Most of the prophetic subjects and terms have been appropriated by them so that their very mention connects with some false religion.

Jesus continually used the term *kingdom of heaven*. The gospel was first called the gospel of the kingdom. The disciples went everywhere preaching the kingdom. It is the only subject on which Jesus taught systematically. In the churches it is now a forgotten subject—not taught, not understood, seldom, if ever, mentioned.

The kingdom is the chief subject of the teaching of one of the biggest false religions. Any mention of the kingdom instantly connects with that movement. When the church ceased to preach so vital a truth as the kingdom, false teachers took it up.

Jesus saw this same situation developing in the whole field of the prophetic Scriptures. What happened on a small scale when there was no special inducement will develop on a large scale when perfect conditions for it prevail.

Perfect conditions for the rise of any number of false teachers will be with us when prophecy begins to be fulfilled on the grand scale that is indicated for the end of the age. The times will be intense; everything will be at the maximum—the greatest advances of science, the greatest destructive power in the hands of wicked people, the greatest war of all time threatening, the greatest activity in the forces of the heavens, especially in the evil spirit world.

The most sensational and unexpected changes will come. Everything may be expressed in extremes. Exaggeration will be almost impossible, and with it all, the most marvelous and miraculous prophetic fulfillments.

If the churches had prepared for this by having a good working knowledge of the prophetic Scriptures—the part that has been left out through the years—they could reap a harvest of souls. There is no miracle in the Bible more sensational than prophecy when it is being fulfilled. God has provided the church with its greatest opportunity for evangelism, and the church is giving it over to false christs. Jesus points out one telling characteristic of a false religion: it says, "I am," or "I am Christ."

### How to Tell a False Religion

A false religion cannot always be detected by its advertised doctrines, but it can quite readily be spotted by its attitude toward other churches. Today there are many evangelical churches with slightly varying beliefs and forms, yet there is but one brotherhood. Such evangelical churches get together for fellowship and revivals, and there are places where they all meet on common ground. But each false religion says, "I am." False religions claim to be the only right way and are separate from the brotherhood. Concerning such, Jesus said, "Go ye not therefore after them."

A favorite place for false religions to begin and to get a following is the radio, which has many advantages. On the radio anyone who has a post office box and the money to pay for the broadcast can put up a good front. Prophecy has always been more or less a racket. The theme of such false teachers is "The time draweth near."

One radio program, a well-financed chain broadcast, came on the air talking about the coming of Christ. Its preacher claimed to be the only depository of truth, but he chose to divulge the truth only in very small amounts. In order to get more information, one had to write to him. The whole thing sounded like another one of those new religions that at the start does not reveal its true nature.

But this radio preacher disclosed his true nature once or twice, for in dealing very hurriedly with the seven periods of church history in Revelation 2 and 3, he said the seven churches did not refer to the ordinary church as we think of it, but to some special church which he did not name. Unwittingly he brought out a truth which we would do well to consider and which will help to identify false religions and false teachers—deceivers, as Jesus called them.

By means of seven typical churches, Revelation tells in advance the whole history of the church. It is not a very flattering story, for the churches seem to have produced more tares than wheat. Sometimes they have been torn by internal strife; sometimes they have had a good name on the outside and at the same time were spiritually dead on the inside. On the other hand, there have been times of great revival and spiritual power.

It should be noted, however, that these characteristics of each of the seven churches in each age are only the dominant ones. Once a certain kind of church starts, it continues to the end of the age, when there will be in the world all kinds of churches—churches like Ephesus, Smyrna, Pergamos, and others. The Philadelphia Church—evangelistic, missionary, entering every open door—will continue until the end of the age; but the Laodicean Church will dominate the scene and will characterize the last period of church history.

When a religious movement claims to be the only true church, setting itself apart from all regular churches and claiming to be the sole custodian of truth, that church is false because it is not one of the seven churches. Its history will not fit the revealed history of the church.

Jesus said that where God sows good seed, Satan sows tares. Thus you can tell a true church by the tares. False religions have no "false teachers" within them. They have no trouble with apostasy, for everybody conforms and nobody has any other ideas than those taught by the church.

It is possible to recognize a true church by its shortcomings, because in Revelation we have a prophecy of those shortcomings. The Laodicean Church is an apostate church, not a false church. An apostate church is not a church whose members are all apostate, but one whose leaders are apostate. However, there is still an appeal to the individual members. Thus Paul speaks of "a falling away." But what false religion would admit a falling away?

In the Olivet Discourse Jesus is not talking about apostasy in the true church, but about new movements which are not and never were true churches. These do not fit into any revealed church history. They are deceivers. In modernism there are many sincere people who would be saved if the right approach could be made, but false religions hold their victims in the grasp of Satan.

## The Churches Are Responsible

The power of these false teachers lies in the fact that the churches are not giving the people the truth which they ought to have.

I once knew a man who discovered in the Bible the truth of the return of Christ. Going to his pastor, he asked him about the return. But his pastor made light of it and said the return referred only to Christ's coming into one's heart. This did not satisfy the young man, so he continued to wonder about Christ's return. Then there came to town a group of people preaching the Second Coming of Christ. Immediately the man became interested, for these were things he wanted to know. Since his church

could not enlighten him, he joined the new group.
Yet from start to finish, it was a false religion;
for although they preached Christ and "the time
draweth near," they denied Christ's deity as well
as almost every basic Christian belief, and were
against all churches. When they got through with
the Second Coming of Christ, one would hardly
recognize it as a Bible doctrine.

If the churches instructed their people in the
truth, situations like this could not happen. The
strength of false religions results from the failure
of the church to teach the whole Bible. Church
people are not ready for the events of the end
of this age. Yet when these events come suddenly
upon us, we will not have time to instruct our
own people. False teachers will have a field day
and will deceive many.

When Jesus said, "Take heed that no man deceive you," He was speaking not to the world but
to His own—to the church. We expect the world
to be deceived, but churches are also in danger.
It is in the churches that deceivers get their victims. The way to combat this danger is to instruct
the people. People who know are not deceived.
God said, "My people are destroyed for lack of
knowledge" (Hos. 4:6).

### "I Am Christ"

Each special time has its own set of false
christs, and their message is geared to the times.
In this first sign, which is a sign of the approaching
resurrection, Jesus specifies that they will say,
"I am Christ." It seems strange that there should
come so many people saying, "I am Christ." It
seems that the claims of one would offset the
claims of another. If we apply these words to conditions as they are now, we would have to assume

that Jesus meant to say merely that these false teachers would claim to represent Him.

However, there may develop a new situation undreamed of before it arises. Satan is interested in religion; he wants to be worshipped. Satan intends to be, in fact, the god of this world. He has principalities and powers in heavenly places.

The times that Jesus was talking about are not normal times. We are not dealing with business as usual. The powers of the heavens will be shaken. Perhaps we should look for a very literal fulfillment of this prophecy.

The only defense against false teaching is truth, but truth is a preventative, not always a cure. Our experience with present-day false religions would lead us to the conclusion that false doctrine is like a disease germ; it sets up a mental block to truth. A person once infected is very difficult to reach. It seems as if one simply cannot get through to him.

Truth is the only answer to false teaching, but *truth has to get there first.* Usually the church is too late. False religions are first on the job.

Jesus warned, "Go ye not therefore after them." This warning would lead us to expect that many will go after them; following false religions, in fact, will be the trend. The road into a false religion is usually a one-way street; there is no return. Only a few find their way back.

## Wars and Rumors of Wars

### MATTHEW 24

4 And Jesus answered and said unto them, Take heed that no man deceive you.

5 For many shall come in my name, saying, I am Christ; and shall deceive many.

6 And ye shall hear of wars and rumours of

wars: see that ye be not troubled: for all these things must come to pass, but the end is not yet.

We have had two so-called world wars, but the whole world was not involved in either, and there was no worldwide crisis or worldwide threat of destruction. Jesus was not talking about normal world conditions or even normal wars. There have been only a few weeks in the history of the world when there was no war anywhere. In order for wars and rumors of wars to be a sign, they must be different from anything which has ever happened before, or must be on a more universal scale.

It is difficult to imagine conditions that would bring about such a situation. We have in the world just one large country whose admitted ambition is to conquer the world. This country is one of the two most powerful nations in the world. It has a political doctrine called Communism which it can use to dominate and enslave people of other countries. This nation manages to supply arms and ammunition to other countries from where the rumors of wars come. It is not in itself a fulfillment of prophecy, but it might be a big factor in the terror that will engulf the world when the big showdown comes. Anticipating this, Jesus said, "Be not terrified."

This would indicate that the coming world crisis will be on a scale that will cause terror throughout the world. Any attempt on the part of one nation to conquer the world would fulfill this prophecy if that nation had so prepared for the day of conquest that it could start trouble in every part of the world at once. Jesus was talking about something that we might call ultimate or final, a world situation that is so serious that nothing could be worse. He is talking about a matter when one of two things must happen: prophecy will be fulfilled, or the world will be destroyed.

When we arrive at that point in time, then we may expect, first that something will happen to prevent the destruction of the world and to bring about world stability, and second, a large amount of prophecy will be fulfilled. There is more prophecy to be fulfilled during the time indicated by the expression "the end is not yet" than is usually realized. These are amazing prophecies that could change not only the whole world but the church as well. In this fantastic, almost impossible, situation that will bring about the fulfillment of this prophecy, Communism must be looked upon as a possible agent. Jesus packed so much into these three verses that only the events themselves will bring out their true meaning.

The fact that there has been a great return of the Jews to their land and a return of the land to productivity makes almost imperative the fulfillment of other prophecies which must accompany these things. Therefore we are driven to the conclusion that Communism will be God's agent in fulfilling the prophecies concerning the wars and rumors of wars. This will spark the fulfillment of so much prophecy in a very literal way that it will become a great religious situation. The fact that prophecy has been fulfilled will become common knowledge throughout the world.

## Commotions

Luke adds an important word. He says, "When ye shall hear of wars and commotions, be not terrified." Commotions are not wars or rumors of wars. They are internal troubles such as Communists produce in every country which they can dominate. The dictionary definition of the Greek word for "commotions" is instability. It is translated "confusion" and "tumult" in other places. In describing the same situation Habakkuk uses the words violence, iniquity, grievance, spoiling, strife, contention, and wrong judgment.

There seems to be an unwritten rule of interpretation that prophetic *events* take place in Bible lands, but certain *conditions* may apply to the whole world. The wars that are involved specifically in prophecy will probably take place in Bible lands.

The Arabs may "kill the goose that lays the golden eggs." They are putting so high a price on their oil that their lands may become very attractive to other countries. They may be bringing destruction on themselves by storing up so much wealth. There is trouble ahead for the Middle East, and this trouble could plunge the whole world into chaos. Some of the events that the prophets foresaw happening in the Middle East such as the building of Babylon, to mention only one, could not very well happen in an Arab-controlled country. It is almost certain that the Arabs will lose ownership of a great deal of the territory they now hold. So much wealth and power will not be overlooked by a country such as Russia. A war in the Middle East over the possession of oil wells would cause commotions in many parts of the world.

It is possible that we should take note of the way Jesus expressed that truth concerning wars and rumors of wars, or commotions. The three Gospel writers—Matthew, Mark, and Luke—who record this message, vary the details somewhat. None of them records the entire discourse, but there is one place where they all agree without any variation. Jesus did not say, there shall be wars and rumors of wars. He said, "Ye shall hear of wars and rumours of wars."

The question arises: Whom did Jesus mean by "ye"? There seem to be some people who will not exactly experience those wars, but who will only hear of them. In His Olivet Discourse Jesus always spoke to the people He was talking about—Christians being persecuted, Jews fleeing from Jerusalem, people looking for the coming of Christ, or people living in a country that is especially favored.

There are other prophecies involving the same time. The church will be especially active; the gospel must go forth to all nations. The false christs which Jesus mentioned must have a place to operate. The United States is one of the bases from which Christianity will spread around the world. There are other countries emerging where the churches are catching the vision of world evangelization. It is possible that people in these countries will only hear of the wars and commotions. We who are living in the United States now may think we are passing through hard times, but they are not as hard as those experienced by people in many other parts of the world. Jesus was possibly speaking with a great deal of precision when He said, "Ye shall hear."

It should also be noted that this time of trouble is brief. This is the background for Antichrist. He will save the world from the nation which is trying to conquer the world, and will bring about a profound peace, so secure that all the money that is now being spent by the military can be used for the enrichment of the people. It is almost impossible to imagine what this will mean to the living standards of the world. This whole process will be so sensational that it should not be difficult to recognize Antichrist when he actually becomes the savior of the world.

Another important feature of prophecy should

be noted here. The Bible makes a very sharp distinction between events before and after the Rapture. Before the Rapture there is peace and prosperity. After the Rapture that all ends, and the world is plunged into judgment. Paul expressed it in these words, "When they shall say, peace and safety, then sudden destruction cometh upon them." Peace and safety come before the Rapture, and sudden destruction comes after the Rapture. Revelation says that God will take peace from the earth. He cannot take peace from the earth unless there is peace on the earth.

Great and wealthy cities like Babylon will be built during the time of peace and safety. The destruction will come afterwards. The result of the wars and commotions that Jesus mentioned is not the Great Day of Judgment; they are only the prelude to the rise of Antichrist. Jesus was careful to add, "Be not terrified, for the end [of the age] is not yet."

## The Chaldean

It would appear from all prophecies that Antichrist will be a sensational character beyond anything the world has ever seen, or that anyone has ever envisioned. It may therefore be reasonably supposed that the conditions out of which Antichrist proceeds will also be sensational beyond anything which anyone has ever envisioned. Only one prophet in the Old Testament saw these conditions in detail. Daniel merely says that there arose another little horn. Habakkuk starts with the conditions that produce the little horn. A man cannot simply rise up, take over a country, and start conquering the world except under very unusual circumstances.

What Habakkuk saw was so unbelievable that

I hesitate to put it in words for fear of ridicule.
Habakkuk felt the same way. He objected to what
he saw; he did not want to write it. He complained
to God about it. Then he said, "I will stand upon
my watch, and set me upon the tower, and watch
and see what he [God] will answer to my com-
plaint." (This is the meaning of his words.) Habakkuk wanted God to change the program, rather
than to publish it. The Lord answered him, but
the answer was not what Habakkuk expected.

### HABAKKUK 2

2 And the Lord answered me, and said, Write
the vision, and make it plain upon tables, that he
may run that readeth it.

3 For the vision is yet for an appointed time,
but at the end it shall speak, and not lie: though
it tarry, wait for it; because it will surely come,
it will not tarry.

*"Write the message and make it plain."* Few
prophecies in the Bible are so strongly emphasized.
Habakkuk has a special place in the time of the
end. His book contains vital information found no-
where else. Instead of beginning his prophecy at
the time of the appearance of Antichrist, as the
others do, Habakkuk starts *before* the rise of Antichrist.

Prophecy has a special place in the program
of God. It is God's prepared weapon against Satan
in the day of Satan's power. No miracle in the
Bible is as sensational as prophecy when it is being
fulfilled. All of Satan's power and signs and lying
wonders will but serve to enforce God's claims
when they are fulfilling His Word.

God has no other way. He has staked everything
on His revealed Word. But to make His plan work,
God must have messengers. They must be instructed before they can instruct others.

*"That he may run that readeth it."* To run is

to proclaim a message. In those days there were
no means of communication except by word of
mouth. The king sent messengers, or runners, to
inform the people of his wishes.

### ZECHARIAH 2

3 And, behold, the angel that talked with me
went forth, and another angel went out to meet
him,

4 And said unto him, Run. . . .

Daniel saw this situation, the time when prophecy would be unsealed, because its time had
come. "Many shall run to and fro and knowledge
shall be increased." Merely running does not increase knowledge. Those who run must have a
message. They must teach.

Knowledge will be increased because the Bible
will be opened up as never before. God has kept
in reserve a vast storehouse of information so vital
that it will shake the world, even in the face of
Antichrist. But knowledge is not increased automatically. It takes teachers. Somebody has to
proclaim it. Many will run.

Habakkuk has the message that will speed the
messengers forth. This is the first detailed prophecy to be fulfilled. It will start the ball rolling.

*"For the vision is yet for an appointed time."*
But in the end, that is, in the end time, it shall
speak. This prophecy is written especially for a
certain time. It will not take its place in God's
plan till that time comes. Then watch out! for it
will shake the church as well as the world. If it
seems to tarry, watch, for it will come on time.

What is this vision that will be so important
in the time of fulfillment? The first two chapters
of Habakkuk have only one subject: Antichrist.

### HABAKKUK 2

4 Behold, his soul which is lifted up is not

upright in him: but the just shall live by his faith.

5 Yea also, because he transgresseth by wine, he is a proud man, neither keepeth at home, who enlargeth his desire as hell, and is as death, and cannot be satisfied, but gathereth unto him all nations, and heapeth unto him all people.

*He is a proud man.* Habakkuk uses no symbols. The book is a poem and at times a certain poetic license is used, such as:

### HABAKKUK 3

8 Thou didst ride upon thine horses and thy chariots of salvation.

Habakkuk does not repeat word for word what the other prophets have said, but he says the same things in his own words, sometimes adding details not found elsewhere. He starts with world conditions, goes from there to the rise of a particular nation, and ends with a man. The man becomes the central figure. In this respect he is like the other prophets.

*"Neither keepeth he at home."* This is explained by the rest of the verse. It does not mean that he goes out nights; it means that he is not content to be the dictator of only one country. He is ambitious. He wants to rule all countries. He raises an army and starts out. It may not take much of an army at the start, because he will have satanic power and possibly help from sources not visible now.

Twice, Germany has tried to become a world power, and other nations would try if they had any promise of success. Antichrist will succeed because, among other things, he will seem to be a savior of the world.

### Communism

Now we will turn to the first chapter and take it from the beginning.

## HABAKKUK 1

1 The burden which Habakkuk the prophet did see.

2 O Lord, how long shall I cry, and thou wilt not hear! even cry out unto thee of violence, and thou wilt not save!

3 Why dost thou shew me iniquity, and cause me to behold grievance? for spoiling and violence are before me: and there are that raise up strife and contention.

4 Therefore the law is slacked, and judgment doth never go forth: for the wicked doth compass about the righteous; therefore wrong judgment proceedeth.

Habakkuk here describes what he saw that caused him so much concern. At first it was not a man or even a country, but a condition, a situation or a system, that was spreading itself over the world, causing great misery. Notice the words Habakkuk uses to describe this new kind of conquest. Violence, iniquity, grievance, spoiling, strife, contention—these are the very words you would use to describe Communism. It starts with violence, using riots, strikes, uprisings, plots, murders—in fact, every known means of undermining legitimate governments.

That is the first phase of their cold war. The next phase is the confiscation of property. The people are robbed (spoiled) of their holdings, put through rigged court trials, and sent to concentration camps. Their accusers are their judges so there is no such thing as a fair trial. It would be difficult to put into words, even today, a more accurate or concise statement of what happens when the Communist gangsters take over a country. It has happened over and over again and is still going on.

The law is slacked, judgment never goes forth, the wicked compass about the righteous, and wrong judgment, or complete injustice, prevails.

This has happened in so many places that we have lost all count. Whole countries, once happy and prosperous, are lost behind the Iron Curtain. Habakkuk saw this situation spreading like a cancerous sore over the entire world until it seemed to him that the entire world would be lost and God's program of redemption would be brought to an abrupt end. (This is what nearly everybody will think before it is over.)

To Habakkuk the world was becoming totally dark, with no possibility of the light of God ever shining through. Yet, what Habakkuk saw is exactly what has happened in country after country. Every year new territory is added to the Communist world program. But we only slow it down; we do not stop it. The terror that Jesus mentioned, caused by world wars and commotions, would be upon us if just one country got out of control, anywhere in the world.

Habakkuk was dealing with a worldwide situation. Now, for the first time since Habakkuk, any war anywhere could bring on a terrifying condition. We got quite concerned about some guns in Cuba aimed at us; but the difference between guns in Cuba and guns in Russia is only about fifteen minutes.

The alternate to being Red is what Habakkuk saw coming. The crisis, when it comes, will be a time of final decision. It will change things as they never have been changed before. This is especially true of the church, and that is why special messengers will be needed.

The only people who can witness in a time like this are people who know what God intends to do—people who understand the prophetic Scriptures. It is hard to put this in words because there are no words to express an experience that has never been faced before by the world or by the church.

## HABAKKUK 1

5 Behold ye among the heathen, and regard, and wonder marvellously: for I will work a work in your days, which ye will not believe, though it be told you.

People have the impression that God never will do anything; but that is not the case. When the time comes God will act.

When God speaks, He speaks to or for the benefit of His people. At the time of this prophecy, God's people are among the nations (called the heathen in the Old Testament). It is a mistake to think that all Old Testament prophecy is only about the Jews. The prophets deal with the whole world, including the New Testament saints. God does not have two separate programs, one for the Jews and one for the rest of the world. He has one program which includes the Jews, the saints, and the world.

"In your days" means that this relief from oppression, or the threat of it, will come in the normal lifetime of the people who are the victims. Jesus put it in another way. He said, "This generation shall not pass till all these things be fulfilled." However, it will be so unexpected that they will be literally stupefied by astonishment. If they did not see it, they would not believe it.

One reason why this will be so unbelievable is that Antichrist's coming is after the working of Satan. Satan will give him his throne and power and great authority. Nothing short of this could cope with the weapons that are in the hands of the nations today.

We have been shown the background; now comes the event. This is what Daniel saw: the rise of the little horn.

## HABAKKUK 1

6 For, lo, I raise up the Chaldeans, that bitter and hasty nation, which shall march through the breadth of the land, to possess the dwelling places that are not theirs.

7 They are terrible and dreadful: their judgment and their dignity shall proceed of themselves.

Now we are dealing with (1) a nation and (2) a man. As to the nation, Daniel told the general location and Habakkuk the character of the people. An important point to remember is: Daniel, Ezekiel and Habakkuk all start with the land and end with a man. We have already noted this in Daniel.

Ezekiel also starts with the land, the land of Magog (Ezek. 38:2), but soon the land is forgotten and only the man is in view.

The land is important only as a starting place for Antichrist. He must start with a small country. Daniel calls it a LITTLE Horn. (The ten horns are nations.) But he soon becomes more stout than his fellows.

Habakkuk starts with a nation which he calls the Chaldeans. The prophets used historical names when they did not know the final names. The ancient country became a type of the final one. However, it is not the ancient country but the final one that Habakkuk describes.

*"I will raise up the Chaldeans, that bitter and hasty nation."* "They are called hasty as being vehement and impetuous in attack and rapid in movement." *Pulpit Commentary.* The Germans had a name for it: Blitzkrieg—lightning war.

*"Which shall march through the breadth of the land,"* or "which marcheth through the breadths of the earth." This explains their general character. This is what they are prone to do.

## DANIEL 8

9 And out of one of them came forth a little

horn, which waxed exceeding great, toward the south, and toward the east, and toward the pleasant land.

Antichrist will move in three directions—south, east, and toward Palestine. To do this, he would have to start in the northwest.

### HABAKKUK 1

8 Their horses also are swifter than the leopards, and are more fierce than the evening wolves: and their horsemen shall spread themselves [bear themselves proudly], and their horsemen shall come from far; they shall fly as the eagle that hasteth to eat.

The Revised Version uses the plural (they) down to the tenth verse, and then changes to the singular (he). The Hebrew is singular after the sixth verse. We are dealing with a nation and a man, the man becoming more important all the time until finally the nation disappears and the man becomes a world figure.

"[His] horsemen . . . fly." They come by air with great speed, and they come from far. The question could arise: How far is far? Distances on earth are becoming very short. We have reached the moon and are looking out into space. Now the moon is not very far. Satan is the prince of the power of the air. He has principalities and powers (organized governments). We may soon find out just what is meant by the power of the air.

It is this seemingly supernatural element in the rise of Antichrist that will make all the difference. His "horsemen" come by air; that makes them airmen. They come not only from a great distance but with extreme speed. This would have to be speed in comparison with enemy planes and missiles. Today that would be almost supernatural speed because we are reaching the limits of human speed.

Daniel says Antichrist will destroy wonderful things. The wonderful things are here, but to destroy them would require something still more wonderful. The United States and Russia have reached a stalemate; neither one can destroy the other and still remain intact. Both would be destroyed because they are about equal in strength. In time other nations may reach the same equality.

But Antichrist will be superior to such an extent that there will be no defense. There is a significance in the simile, "As the eagle that hasteth to eat." An eagle swoops down from the sky at great speed. It drops almost straight down on its prey.

### HABAKKUK 1

9 They shall come all for violence: their faces shall sup up as the east wind, and they shall gather the captivity as the sand.

10 And they shall scoff at the kings, and the princes shall be a scorn unto them: they shall deride every strong hold; for they shall heap dust, and take it.

He will come upon his enemies with a great show of violence. His face will look toward the east. That is the meaning of "he shall sup up as the east wind." That eastward movement is again noted. It seems to put the nation somewhere in the western part of Europe.

"[He] shall scoff at the. kings." Nations with atomic power will present no problem to him, for he will have a superior weapon. A hundred years ago that might have been a bomber, but what would it be today? It is impossible to conceive such power in the hands of one man. Antichrist would have no means of developing such power, or weapons of that magnitude, without being detected. The only alternative is that his coming is

after the working of Satan with all power and
signs and lying wonders.

"[He] shall heap dust, and take it." The R.V.
is stronger: "[He] shall heap *up* dust, and take
it." He will take a stronghold by throwing dust
at it! The best the commentators can do with
that is to say that he will throw a pile of dust
up and hide behind it. But the commentaries
were written before anybody knew anything about
radio-active dust.

This is not a defensive measure. Antichrist is
on the march. He is conquering whole countries.
He is "gathering the captivity as the sand." Dust
is his weapon of conquest. Today scientists could
tell us the exact nature of that dust. They are
trying to make it. If his horsemen come from
far, they may bring the dust with them, and that
will give Antichrist absolute control. The empire
that he will set up will eventually include the four
empires of Daniel, but his influence will be worldwide and that influence will be great.

### HABAKKUK 1

11 Then shall his mind change, and he shall
pass over, and offend, imputing this his power
unto his god.

"Then shall his mind change." There are other
translations: "Then he sweepeth on as the wind."
He is like a tempestuous wind that sweeps all
before it. It corresponds to Daniel's prediction that
he will pull up three horns by the roots.

"Imputing this his power unto his god." Again
Daniel makes a similar statement. Daniel says
it will be "not by his own power." His power comes
from Satan. Eventually this will be acknowledged.
Revelation says they will worship the dragon which
gave power to the beast.

Up to this point God has been explaining to Habakkuk how He will overcome the curse that has been spreading itself over the earth. Now Habakkuk speaks.

### HABAKKUK 1

12 Art thou not from everlasting, O Lord my God, mine Holy One? we shall not die. O Lord, thou hast ordained them for judgment; and, O mighty God, thou hast established them for correction.

13 Thou art of purer eyes than to behold evil, and canst not look on iniquity: wherefore lookest thou upon them that deal treacherously, and holdest thy tongue when the wicked devoureth the man that is more righteous than he?

14 And makest men as the fishes of the sea, as the creeping things, that have no ruler over them?

15 They take up all of them with the angle, they catch them in their net, and gather them in their drag: therefore they rejoice and are glad.

16 Therefore they sacrifice unto their net, and burn incense unto their drag; because by them their portion is fat, and their meat plenteous.

17 Shall they therefore empty their net, and not spare continually to slay the nations?

*"We shall not die."* Habakkuk identifies himself with God's people and speaks as though he were living at the time of fulfillment. This is quite common practice. Our hope, says Habakkuk, is in the fact that God is from everlasting, and even though things may seem hopeless at times, His purpose cannot fail.

*"Thou hast established [him] for correction."* The Chaldean (Antichrist) is a rod in God's hand to correct the injustices that Habakkuk saw and complained about. Afterward, God will deal with Antichrist. Isaiah calls Antichrist the Assyrian and

says, "O Assyrian, the rod of mine anger, and the staff in their [the Assyrians'] hand is mine indignation" (Isa. 10:5).

God will also punish Israel by the same rod. That is what Isaiah is especially concerned about. The principle is the same: God uses one evil power to punish another one. Isaiah says, "He thinketh not so." Antichrist does not realize that he is carrying out God's program and that God is using him to carry out His own purpose.

Habakkuk's question "Why?" is the question we all ask. Why does God allow these things? We get the answer, as Habakkuk did, by looking at the goal. This goal is stated in 2:14: "For the earth shall be filled with the knowledge of the glory of the Lord, as the waters cover the sea."

Now follows a summary of the activities of Antichrist to the time of the end, when he will gather all nations against the Lord. The nations are like fish. Antichrist empties his net, then goes out for more. "He gathereth unto him all nations, and heapeth unto him all people" (2:5)

This is the harvest. God allows evil to run its full course and come to its natural harvest. Then it will be judged. So, Habakkuk concludes, "The Lord is in his holy temple: let all the earth keep silence before him" (2:20).

## Conclusion

To identify Antichrist it is essential that we do more than look for a man, even a very special kind of man. We must take into consideration the world conditions out of which this man comes. This is Habakkuk's contribution to the cause. He starts not with the man, but with the conditions that produce the man. He sees the world facing chaos.

Today statesmen freely predict that we are in danger of a return to barbarism. Conditions in the world continually worsen. At the last minute a man will rise up with peculiar power. He will bring the world back to its senses by a power which seems to be supernatural. This man will not be satisfied with one nation, but will "heap unto him all peoples."

## CHAPTER 6

# The Man of Sin

II THESSALONIANS 2
1 Now we beseech you, brethren, by [concerning] the coming of our Lord Jesus Christ, and by our gathering together unto him. . .

The church at Thessalonica was established by Paul on his second missionary journey. His preaching aroused such violent controversy in the synagogues that the opposing Jewish faction brought him before the city magistrate, charging him with fomenting insurrection against Caesar. Paul's friends were placed under bond, and to protect their own security they sent him away from the city.

Paul taught the Thessalonians about the Second Coming of Christ and the rise of Antichrist which would precede it. In his letters to the Thessalonians Paul did not repeat to any extent his teachings, but simply reminded them of what he had taught them. It is apparent from this letter that the Thessalonians were applying Paul's teaching concerning the coming of Christ to the events that were happening in their day. Some of them thought that the Rapture was near at hand because of what was happening. Paul told them that that was not the case—that some other things must happen first.

The particular phase of the coming of Christ that Paul was talking about is the Rapture, our gathering together unto Him. Paul said that that day would not come till after the appearance of the man of sin that we call Antichrist and the falling away from the faith on the part of many professing believers.

### II THESSALONIANS 2

2 That ye be not soon shaken in mind, or be troubled, neither by spirit, nor by word, nor by letter as from us, as that the day of Christ is at hand.

The "day of Christ" in this verse should be read "day of the Lord." The day of the Lord usually refers to the time between the Rapture and the Second Coming of Christ, a period of about 10 1/2 years. Sometimes it refers to a part of that time such as the seven last plagues of Revelation.

### II THESSALONIANS 2

3 Let no man deceive you by any means: for that day shall not come, except there come a falling away first, and that man of sin be revealed, the son of perdition.

A "falling away" may be read "the apostasy." The apostasy is a great falling away from the faith which will come in the last days just before the return of Christ for His church. Peter puts it in these words:

### II PETER 3

3 Knowing this first, that there shall come in the last days scoffers, walking after their own lusts,

4 And saying, Where is the promise of his com-

ing? for since the fathers fell asleep, all things
continue as they were from the beginning of the
creation.

We have had during the last fifty years or so
what has been considered by many an apostasy.
Many churches have departed from the faith. It
is a situation called modernism or liberalism. The
sacrifice of Christ for the sins of the world has
been played down, almost to the point of denying
the very deity of Christ. In fact, many semi-
nary teachers believe the "God is dead" theory
and teach it. Young seminarians follow these
teachers and as a result churches do not preach
or even believe their own doctrines. This seems
like a fulfillment of this prophecy, but there is
one thing lacking: the doctrine of the Second Coming of Christ has not been a big factor; it has
not been a point of great controversy. The doctrine
of the coming of Christ has been disregarded but
not scoffed at. The church hymns are full of the
subject, and the rituals contain references to it.

There is coming a great worldwide revival. This
revival will be sparked by the fulfillment of prophecy. There will be so many miraculous fulfillments
that the people generally will be looking for the
coming of Christ. Many of these signs will revolve
around Antichrist. Christ will not come to receive
His church at the height of this evangelistic fervor.
There must be a testing. Things will quiet down.
The Lord will not come; the miracles and signs
will cease, and a great feeling of security will
spread over the world. Many people will say,
"Well, the preachers were wrong. The Lord did
not come after all." It is when they think not that
the Son of Man cometh.

This falling away will immediately precede the
revelation of the man of sin. Paul talked about
two things, the coming of Antichrist and the rev-

elation of Antichrist. They are not the same. Antichrist will come and operate for a number of years before the Rapture. He will not be revealed as Satan until after the Rapture. At the Rapture Antichrist will be killed, and Satan will take over his body and reign in person on the earth. It will seem like a resurrection. From that time on, the world will know that he is Antichrist; that is his revelation. Paul speaks of him whose coming is after the working of Satan. He must come before he is revealed.

## II THESSALONIANS 2

4 Who opposeth and exalteth himself above all that is called God, or that is worshipped; so that he as God sitteth in the temple of God, shewing himself that he is God.

Here Paul gives us one of the principal identifying marks of Antichrist. He will exalt himself above God until finally he will set himself up as an object of worship in the temple. This is probably what Daniel and Jesus referred to as the abomination of desolation. This, of course, cannot happen until after the temple is built. Paul gives us the story from beginning to end. Antichrist will be a god and eventually become an object of worship in the temple.

## II THESSALONIANS 2

6 And now ye know what withholdeth that he might be revealed in his time.

7 For the mystery of iniquity doth already work: only he who now letteth will let, until he be taken out of the way.

8 And then shall that Wicked be revealed, whom the Lord shall consume with the spirit of his mouth, and shall destroy with the brightness of his coming.

The complete teaching of Paul concerning Antichrist is not reported in this chapter. Paul simply states enough in his letter to remind the Thessalonians of what he had taught them. Antichrist will be restrained. There are two powers working —the power of Satan in Antichrist and the power of the Holy Spirit working through the church. There are some things that Antichrist cannot do. There is no suggestion anywhere in prophecy that Antichrist will be able to hinder the spread of the gospel prior to the Rapture. After the Rapture Antichrist will be revealed as Satan and will be unrestrained.

*"For the mystery of iniquity doth already work: only he who now letteth will let, until he be taken out of the way."* This verse is sometimes interpreted to mean that the Holy Spirit will hinder the operation of Satan until He is taken out of the world when He "goes up with the church" at the resurrection. This is a strange interpretation of a verse which does not mention the world or make any reference to it. The Holy Spirit will never be taken out of the world; He has been in the world ever since the Spirit of God moved on the face of the waters (Gen. 1:2). Paul does not say that the Holy Spirit will be taken out of the world, but only out of the way of the mystery of iniquity.

The word "let" in this verse means to hinder. This verse is an enigma, purposely so. It was meant to be understood by the faithful, but not by their enemies. In Thessalonica Paul was given a hard time by the authorities. He knew that the church there was in a precarious position; undoubtedly there would be spies in every service. Paul's letter would be carefully scrutinized to find evidence against the church. Paul had to state this somewhat dangerous truth in such a way that the church would understand it, and the spies would not.

When Antichrist begins to operate, the mystery of iniquity will be very much at work, but there will be a hindrance; this hindrance is the Holy Spirit working through the church until a certain time. That time we know to be the Rapture. At that time all hindrances to Satan will be removed, and he will have full license to persecute the saints. The persecution of the saints will come after the Rapture, not before. There are always spots in the world where there is persecution, but a general worldwide persecution will not come before the Rapture.

*"Then shall that Wicked [One] be revealed."* When Antichrist first rises, his identity will not be revealed. The world will not recognize him as Antichrist or the man of sin. Only those who are instructed in the Word and have the enlightenment of the Holy Spirit will recognize him. After the Rapture Antichrist will vigorously persecute the saints, even unto death. They will all recognize him when that is going on. The saints that Antichrist persecutes after the Rapture are people who will be saved after the Rapture. Revelation says that there will be a great number from every kindred, tongue, people, and nation. That persecution will last 3 1/2 years. It is called the great tribulation. Then God's judgments on Antichrist and his kingdom will start in a big way, which will end in the judgment of Antichrist who in Revelation is called the beast.

### REVELATION 19

17 And I saw an angel standing in the sun; and he cried with a loud voice, saying to all the fowls that fly in the midst of heaven, Come and gather yourselves together unto the supper of the great God;

18 That ye may eat the flesh of kings, and the flesh of captains, and the flesh of mighty men, and the flesh of horses, and of them that sit on

them, and the flesh of all men, both free and
bond, both small and great.

19 And I saw the beast, and the kings of the
earth, and their armies, gathered together to make
war against him that sat on the horse, and against
his army.

20 And the beast was taken, and with him the
false prophet that wrought miracles before him,
with which he deceived them that had received
the mark of the beast, and them that worshipped
his image. These both were cast alive into a lake
of fire burning with brimstone.

Paul is making a most important point here.
We must distinguish between the operation of the
man of sin before the Rapture, when the church
is a hindering force, and the unhindered operations
of the "beast" when the church is taken out of
the way. Paul says Antichrist will be revealed in
his time. There is a time for everything. Any prophecy taken out of its time and put in some other
time will always be a misunderstood prophecy.

There are a number of time zones, both before
and after the Rapture, and every prophecy should
be carefully placed in its proper time zone. Paul
speaks of the coming of Antichrist and of his revelation. They are two separate events.

## II THESSALONIANS 2

9 Even him, whose coming is after the working
of Satan with all power and signs and lying wonders.

10 And with all deceivableness of unrighteousness in them that perish; because they received
not the love of the truth, that they might be
saved.

11 And for this cause God shall send them
strong delusion, that they should believe a lie:

12 That they all might be damned who be-
lieved not the truth, but had pleasure in unrighteousness.

*"His coming is after the working of Satan."*
"The coming of the lawless one by the activity
of Satan will be with all power and with pretended
signs and wonders" (RSV). This is a key verse
when we are considering how to recognize Antichrist because Paul is here stating the main feature of the rise of Antichrist. It is at his rise that
he must be recognized by the saints.

The words "all power" in both the King James
and the RSV are somewhat startling. Jesus said,
"All power is given unto me." Antichrist is coming
at a time when the nations have what seems to
be all power—power to destroy the world in a few
minutes. It is the threat of the exercise of this
power that causes the crisis that brings forth Antichrist. The nations have all atomic power; Antichrist has all satanic power. Antichrist will have
a power which will neutralize and render powerless
all atomic weapons. In the end Christ's power
will destroy Antichrist.

The word "lying" modifies both signs and wonders. In that respect the RSV is correct. However,
Antichrist's signs may not be pretended. They will
be deceitful, but the deceit will lie in the fact
that they deceive the world. The signs and wonders
in themselves may be genuine.

Paul says that the people were deceived because they did not have a love of the truth. It
is possible to know the truth and not love the truth.
There are many people eternally lost who are thoroughly acquainted with the truth. Pontius Pilate
knew the truth, but washed his hands of it. In
the last days of this age the truth will be thoroughly
known by most people of the world.

Antichrist will be a man, not Satan. He will
have something extremely spectacular at the start
in order to sell himself to the world, but especially
to the nation that he uses to restore a world empire.

The signs and wonders do not necessarily carry all the way through Antichrist's reign. There were signs and wonders at the birth of Christ, but they were not repeated. There were signs and wonders at Pentecost, but most of them were not repeated. Antichrist's signs and wonders will be for the purpose of deceiving the world, but once he has accomplished that purpose, the signs and wonders may cease.

At the time of his rise there will be a great world crisis, probably due to the fact that the nations are preparing to use atomic power, and Russia will be expected to use her superpower to dominate the world. Antichrist will single-handedly relieve the world of this threat by a demonstration of signs and wonders that shows he has more power than Russia or any other nation that might flex its muscles at that time.

God will have some signs and wonders, but they will be of a spiritual nature. Antichrist's signs and wonders will be of a physical nature, but they will connect directly with the spirit world. The signs and wonders may come directly from outer space where Satan is known to have principalities and powers. This demonstration of power is going to be so spectacular, so sensational, so unexpected that no one who loves the truth could possibly fail to recognize the fulfillment of this prophecy.

Whenever we talk about things of this kind, the question always arises: "Will this happen before the Rapture?" This will not only happen before the Rapture, it will happen some little time before the Rapture. Many of the events and developments that have to come before the Rapture, happen during the reign of Antichrist. These include the building of great cities mentioned before in this book; a crisis in Israel that turns all the Jews back to God—not just to the land; the complete return of the Jews (every last Jew is going back, as reported in the next chapter); the rebuilding of the temple; and a great worldwide evangelistic explosion.

## CHAPTER 7

# Antichrist and the Jews

In Revelation the symbol of Antichrist is a beast. The symbol becomes a name, and the empire of Antichrist is called the Kingdom of the Beast.

Egypt will of necessity be considered a part of that kingdom, but the relationship between Egypt and Antichrist will not always be good. At times there will be actual warfare. Egypt will become very powerful, so powerful in fact that she will have ideas of conquering the world. There will be an Egyptian empire, including a large part of North Africa. There is a direct connection between the prophecies concerning Egypt and the prophecies concerning the return of the Jews. They are going back, for the most part, by way of Egypt.

Antichrist's attitude toward the Jews will probably be evident from the start. It will be the same as Hitler's, except that Antichrist will attempt to destroy all the Jews in the whole world.

It must be remembered that Antichrist is a protégé of Satan, and will carry out Satan's program. Satan's attempt to destroy the Jews is of long standing. A number of times in history the

Jews have narrowly escaped; in fact, the history of Israel is the history of narrow escapes.

In prophecy Esau represents the Arabs, and Jacob, the Jews. Ever since Jacob got the birthright from Esau by trickery, there has been enmity between those two brothers and their descendants. The Jews come down from Jacob, and the Arabs, from Esau (and from Ishmael, another enemy of the Jews).

The history of the Jews is a history of expulsion from one country after another. Whenever Satan gets the upper hand, the Jews are in trouble. This historical fact is implicit in the call of Abram, which was a call to start a new race, and we read in Genesis:

### GENESIS 12

1 Now the Lord had said unto Abram, Get thee out of thy country, and from thy kindred, and from thy father's house, unto a land that I will shew thee:

2 And I will make of thee a great nation, and I will bless thee, and make thy name great; and thou shalt be a blessing:

3 And I will bless them that bless thee, and curse him that curseth thee: and in thee shall all families of the earth be blessed.

There are two items in this call which are of interest to us now. First, a special blessing is pronounced on those people or those nations that are a blessing to Israel. If there ever has been a nation that could claim that blessing, it is the United States. The Jews have prospered in this country from the very beginning, and it has always been a friend of Israel.

England has been a friend of the Jews at times, but to a much lesser extent. It is true that the Balfour Declaration guaranteed the Jews a home in Palestine, but actually England did all she could to prevent the return of the Jews. Anti-Jewish leaders were in control. England's treatment of the Jews during and after the Hitler persecution, when they were trying to escape from the Hitler-controlled countries, is one of the darkest pages in the history of England.

The Jews have a nation today in Palestine solely because of the friendship of the United States. If it had not been for our help, the nation of Israel would have been annihilated long ago.

Among all the nations of history this nation alone has the right to claim this promise in its fullness. This may become a very important truth. The rise of Antichrist will be made possible by a threat of worldwide destruction. The world will be concerned only with survival. Even that will be in doubt. Such a condition will produce paralysis in commerce and trade and in the raising and transportation of food. People will be terrified. The whole world will be involved in this struggle for survival. It will be then that this promise of special blessing will be very precious. Among all the nations of the earth this country will be especially favored in the coming crisis.

The second special feature of the call of Abram involves Antichrist. "I will curse him that curseth thee." Satan will take this as a personal threat. God said, "I will bless *them* that bless thee," but He said, "I will curse *him* that curseth thee." The threat is against a man, and it indicates that a man is going to curse Israel. Here the whole history of Israel is put into one sentence. The climax of this curse will be when Satan's man is dominating the world. From the very start Antichrist will be against the Jews. Previously nations have been concerned only with driving the Jews out of their particular countries; Antichrist's concern will be to annihilate all the Jews in the world.

God's whole future program revolves around Israel. This truth is also expressed in the call of Abram: "In thee shall all families of the earth be blessed." God's entire kingdom program revolves around Israel. When Christ comes again, according to the prophet Zechariah, His feet shall stand upon the Mount of Olives which is before Jerusalem. The Jews will be the nucleus of the new kingdom. If Satan is to win this war and retain control of the earth, he must of necessity destroy all Jews. That would prevent the establishing of the Kingdom of God in the world. This is basic in the program of Satan. His first attempt, when he gets control of the earth, will be to destroy all Jews. This will provoke the greatest crisis in the history of Israel. This particular feature of the character and works of Antichrist will be so prominent that it will be a positive mark of identification.

## A Drama in Three Acts

The much prophesied return of the Jews is a process rather than a single event. The Jews have a threefold relationship: (1) Their relationship to the land; (2) their relationship to God; (3) their relationship to Christ, their Messiah. Consequently there are three steps to the return. It is like a three-act play.

They have a relationship to the land. It is called the Promised Land because God made a covenant with Abraham, giving him this land that it might belong to him and his descendants forever.

GENESIS 17

1 And when Abram was ninety years old and nine, the Lord appeared to Abram, and said unto him, I am the Almighty God, walk before me, and be thou perfect.

2 And I will make my covenant between me and thee, and will multiply thee exceedingly.

3 And Abram fell on his face: and God talked with him, saying,

4 As for me, behold, my covenant is with thee, and thou shalt be a father of many nations.

5 Neither shall thy name any more be called Abram, but thy name shall be Abraham; for a father of many nations have I made thee.

6 And I will make thee exceeding fruitful, and I will make nations of thee, and kings shall come out of thee.

7 And I will establish my covenant between me and thee and thy seed after thee in their generations for an everlasting covenant, to be a God unto thee, and to thy seed after thee.

8 And I will give unto thee, and to thy seed after thee, the land wherein thou art a stranger, all the land of Canaan, for an everlasting possession; and I will be their God.

Abraham was told to walk through this land. Every step was to be an act of possession. Abraham started his journey at Haran which is near the Euphrates River as it crosses the northern part of Syria. When Abraham finally got in the midst of the Promised Land, there was a famine in progress, and Abraham, in order to feed his flocks, had to go all the way into Egypt. Therefore Syria and Egypt became the projected northern and southern boundaries of the Promised Land.

### GENESIS 15

18 In the same day the Lord made a covenant with Abram, saying, Unto thy seed have I given this land, from the river of Egypt unto the great river, the river Euphrates.

The river of Egypt almost has to be the Nile. Some commentators think that the reference is to a stream or creek of Egypt which is nearer

the ancient boundary between Palestine and
Egypt, now totally occupied by Israel. However,
that small stream would not have been known to
Abraham, and perhaps would not, in Abraham's
day, have been called by that name.

The northern boundary was to be the Euphrates
where it crosses Syria. This would take in most
of Syria and all of Lebanon. Other prophecies would
indicate that the Jews will not come into possession
of this much territory until after the Second Coming of Christ. Prophecy does not indicate the exact
boundaries of Israel before the coming of Christ.

One would think that what is happening in
Palestine today would have the whole Christian
world searching the Scriptures to see what bearing
the State of Israel has on the prophecies of the
last days. You would think that the beginning of
the realization of so much prophecy would put the
whole church in a state of expectancy. But nobody
gets excited, not even those who make a special
claim that they believe the whole Bible. WHY?

For one thing, things did not happen as we have
been taught to expect them to. Many people have
thought that the Rapture would come before any
prophecy could be fulfilled. This has been a very
serious error.

Then, too, the details of the return do not seem
to correspond with the prophecy as we have understood it. There are many prophecies concerning
the return of the Jews that are not in sight now.
But it is better to take a second look and find
out exactly what the Bible says than to reject the
prophecies because some things did not happen
the way we thought they would.

The return of the Jews is a very complicated
process. There are so many factors involved, not
the least of which is their attitude toward Christ.
Their attitude toward Christ is, in fact, the con-

trolling factor. There can be no stability in Israel until Christ is King. That is the goal. The Jews will reach that goal in three steps: one is past or in progress; two are yet to come.

Between the first and second steps great changes will take place in the world. Communism will probably almost succeed in its announced intention to take over the world. Relief will come, but the benefit will be only temporary. The next world crisis of importance will be the one that produces Antichrist. The second crisis for Israel will come after that.

It seems strange that so little research has been done on this subject, seeing so much space has been given to it in the Bible. If we brought together all the prophecies concerning the return of the Jews, without an understanding of the order of events, we would have what would seem like a mass of contradictions and confused statements. It is not a simple process. It is not a matter of the Jews packing up and going to Palestine to live happily ever after.

There are three separate situations. If you take prophecies concerning one phase of the return and apply them to another, there will be difficulties. We have to get our bearings and understand the order of events. The return of the Jews from all countries at once is a much more complicated endeavor than their coming out of bondage in Egypt.

## Act I—The Land

The first step in the return of the Jews is not the return of all of the Jews to the land, but the return of the land to the Jews. Before Hitler there were twenty million Jews in the world, scattered over many different countries and having many

different cultures. To weld them into one har-
monious nation would be an order of first magnitude. The first step would be the possession of
the land, but the land was owned by the Turks,
and the Jews were not allowed there in any
numbers. World War I freed the land from the
Turks, but only the persecution of Hitler gave the
Jews the necessary drive to settle the land.

The Jews had no great desire to remove to
Palestine. They were, for the most part, happy
and prosperous in their adopted lands. Many of
them had become rich and powerful. There was
a Zionist movement, but it was opposed by many
Jews. A land of sand and rocks and poverty did
not seem very attractive. Hitler demonstrated to
the Jews that they could not live in permanent
peace and prosperity until they could own their
own land and have their own nation.

As a reward for the invention of TNT by a
Jew, Great Britain was entrusted with a mandate
to establish a Jewish home in Palestine—a home,
not a state. But Great Britain allowed only 75,000
Jews to enter Palestine, then shut off all immigra-
tion in order to appease the Arabs. At the time
Britain was engaged in some empire building in
Southern Arabia and needed the friendship of the
Arabs.

The direct result of World War II was that the
British lost the mandate and the Jews forced their
way into Palestine and established an independent
state. This was the beginning of the fulfillment
of such prophecies as:

### EZEKIEL 34

11 For thus saith the Lord God; Behold, I,
even I, will both search my sheep, and seek them
out.

12 As a shepherd seeketh out his flock in the
day that he is among his sheep that are scattered;

so will I seek out my sheep, and will deliver them
out of all places where they have been scattered
in the cloudy and dark day.

13 And I will bring them out from the people,
and gather them from the countries, and will bring
them to their own land, and feed them upon the
mountains of Israel by the rivers, and in all the
inhabited places of the country.

Before Hitler there were about twenty million
Jews in the world. That many Jews could not find
support in Palestine in its barren state. It has
lain waste for centuries, for only Jews can prosper
there.

Therefore, if the land has to support so many
Jews all at once, some preliminary work would
have to be done. Inasmuch as Palestine would produce only for Jews, there would have to be a partial
return before the whole company of Jews could
be supported. The first crisis produced this preliminary return. It could not fulfill all the prophecy, but it fulfilled some of it.

We have to distinguish between prophecies
about the Jews and prophecies about the land.
Some prophecy concerning the land has been fulfilled by this first part of the return.

The Jews returned to their land, but they did
not return to God. They returned to their language, Hebrew; they returned to their customs;
they returned to their love of the land, but their
attitude toward God did not change. They thought
they did it all in their own power. This is the reason
there has to be a second crisis. It will take more
to turn them to God than it did to turn them
to the land. The next crisis will be greater than
the first, not for the world, possibly, but for the
Jews.

### EZEKIEL 36

1 Also, thou son of man, prophesy unto the

mountains of Israel, and say, Ye mountains of Israel, hear the word of the Lord:
  2  Thus saith the Lord God; Because the enemy
hath said against you, Aha, even the ancient high
places are ours in possession.

Notice that this prophecy is especially concerning the land:

EZEKIEL 36
  8 But ye, O mountains of Israel, ye shall
shoot forth your branches, and yield your fruit to
my people of Israel; for they are at hand to come.

Almost as soon as the Jews started going back,
we began getting glowing reports and pictures
telling how the land was responding. Swamps were
drained, trees were planted, gardens dotted the
landscape, roads were built, cities sprang up; but
there was one complication—the Arabs. They had
been schooled by the British to oppose the Jews.
They did not need much prodding.

The only land available to the Jews was land
nobody wanted—the waste places and the rocky
slopes. The Arabs said, "Aha, even the ancient
high places are ours in possession."

The Jews cannot think of building their temple
as long as a Moslem shrine, the Dome of the Rock,
stands on the site of the Holy of Holies. This opposition of the Arabs will continue till the next crisis.
The prophecy does not correspond to the present
situation. It covers all the time between the first
and second crises. God himself will settle the matter with the Arabs. This will be one of the high
spots of the return. Now the Jews are in Palestine
by their own power.

But when all the Jews return at once under
the power of God, and in complete fulfillment of
the prophecies, a nation born in a day, Arab power
will be destroyed. At present we see only the begin-
nings, but we can trace the future by studying

what the Arabs will do, so first, let us look at
Arab countries and their boasted plans.

### EZEKIEL 35

1 Moreover the word of the Lord came unto
me, saying,

2 Son of man, set thy face against mount Seir,
and prophesy against it,

3 And say unto it, Thus saith the Lord God;
Behold, O mount Seir, I am against thee, and I
will stretch out mine hand against thee, and I
will make thee most desolate.

4 I will lay thy cities waste, and thou shalt be
desolate, and thou shalt know that I am the Lord.

*"Mount Seir."* The Arabs are descendants of
Ishmael and Esau. Esau took a wife of the daughters of Ishmael (Gen. 28:9). In prophecy the Arabs
are always referred to by names applying to Esau
who dwelt in Seir (Deut. 2:4-6).

God says He will lay the land of the Arabs
waste and it will be desolate. It seems that
way now, but the prophecy is concerning a future
punishment. God will lay their land waste because
of what they do to the Jews at the time of their
return. The land could not be laid waste now because it is already waste. You would not notice
much difference. But the Middle East is destined
to become prosperous again. Great cities will be
built and the land will be filled with prosperous
communities. Then this prophecy will take on real
meaning.

Now we have two reasons why God will destroy
the cities of the Arabs. This may seem like a severe
punishment; but the provocation is going to be
very great. The terms of the covenant must be
carried out to the letter: "I will curse him that
curseth thee."

### EZEKIEL 35

5 Because thou hast had a perpetual hatred,

and hast shed the blood of the children of Israel by the force of the sword in the time of their calamity, in the time that their iniquity had an end:

6 Therefore, as I live, saith the Lord God, I will prepare thee unto blood, and blood shall pursue thee: sith thou hast not hated blood, even blood shall pursue thee.

7 Thus will I make mount Seir most desolate, and cut off from it him that passeth out and him that returneth.

8 And I will fill his mountains with his slain men: in thy hills, and in thy valleys, and in all thy rivers, shall they fall that are slain with the sword.

9 I will make thee perpetual desolations, and thy cities shall not return: and ye shall know that I am the Lord.

*"Because thou hast had a perpetual hatred":*

### GENESIS 27

41 And Esau hated Jacob because of the blessing wherewith his father blessed him: and Esau said in his heart, The days of mourning for my father are at hand; then will I slay my brother Jacob.

Esau still has this determination. It has lasted through the years. Edom is another name for the descendants of Esau (Gen. 36:8).

They have had a perpetual hatred. This was expressed in their slogan: "Drive the Jews into the sea." The only reason the Arabs do not do it is because they are not strong enough. If they should try it before the time, they would probably lose more territory. Eventually, they will drive the Jews out, but that will be the second crisis.

*"In the time of their calamity."* The prophet is very specific about the time of this prophecy. It is the time of the iniquity of the end (R.V.)

or, the time their iniquity had an end (A.V.).
Either way, it is the general time of the return.
The Arabs will give them trouble during the first
and second crises. The third crisis is of a different
nature.

Ezekiel 35 deals with what is happening now
and what will happen from now till the second
crisis is resolved. This is prophecy that is actually
being fulfilled now. The time of their calamity
is a time when the Jews are being driven out of
their home countries and have no place to go but
to Egypt.

This prophecy began to be fulfilled as soon as
the Jews started settling in Palestine. In the beginning it was the British more than the Arabs that
caused the distress. From now on it will be Arabs,
the Egyptians, and Antichrist. The prophecy covers the whole time that the Jews are in the process
of returning. After the second crisis, the return
will be complete.

### EZEKIEL 35

10 Because thou hast said, These two nations
and these two countries shall be mine, and we
will possess it; whereas the Lord was there.

What is meant by "whereas the Lord was
there"? God's promises to Israel include prosperity in the land, earthly goods, long life, a plenti-
ful harvest (Deut. 28:1-14). Therefore, if the land
prospered and yielded its fruit in abundance, it
was a sign that the Lord was there. For many
centuries Palestine has been waste. The Lord was
not there. During those years it made no difference
who occupied the land or claimed possession of
it.

But when the Jews took over some of the land,
everything changed. The covenant was about to
be put back into effectiveness. The land was being

made ready for the complete return. It was becoming miraculously productive. The Lord was there. Then, if the Arabs made false claims they would be fighting against God.

*"These two nations and these two countries."* Sometimes we think of Israel as being two countries because they were two nations for a time. There is only one nation now. Still, Palestine is divided into two countries, held by two nations. If the Arabs claimed just the part they now occupy, there would be no immediate crisis; but they claim the whole of Palestine—both countries. They are determined to drive the Jews out of every inch of the land. They say, "It is all ours and we will possess it."

### EZEKIEL 36

3 Therefore prophesy and say, Thus saith the Lord God; Because they have made you desolate, and swallowed you up on every side, that ye might be a possession unto the residue of the heathen, and ye are taken up in the lips of talkers, and are an infamy of the people:

4 Therefore, ye mountains of Israel, hear the word of the Lord God; Thus saith the Lord God to the mountains, and to the hills, to the rivers, and to the valleys, to the desolate wastes, and to the cities that are forsaken, which became a prey and derision to the residue of the heathen that are round about:

5 Therefore thus saith the Lord God; Surely in the fire of my jealousy have I spoken against the residue of the heathen, and against all Idumea, which have appointed my land into their possession with the joy of all their heart, with despiteful minds, to cast it out for a prey.

The time of this prophecy can be fixed. It concerns the land. It is addressed, not to the people, but to the mountains, the hills, the valleys and the rivers. The time, therefore, is before the Jews are in possession of all the land. God is talking about the land that is occupied by their enemies.

However, the Jews have to be occupying some of the land, because the Arabs are planning to cast them out and take over their possessions for a prey. It also says that this is when they are at hand to come. The mass return has not yet taken place.

The time, then, is after the preliminary return and before the great mass return when the Jews will occupy all the land. This is the time we are in now. We are actually seeing this prophecy being fulfilled. We are living between the first and second crises. Every detail is happening exactly as prophesied, even to the actual words of the Arabs.

The enemy has swallowed up the land on every side and has made it desolate. The nations round about are determined to possess the land; so, God speaks out against the nations of the Arabs because they have "appointed my land into their possession with the joy of all their heart, with despiteful minds, to cast it out for a prey." This is what they are planning to do—drive out the Jews and take their land, the land they have worked so hard to redeem. This action will bring about the second crisis. It is while this particular phase of the return of the Jews is in progress that Antichrist will come.

Antichrist may not start the persecution of the Jews immediately after he comes into power. His first problem will be Communism as headed up by Russia. When Antichrist gets through with Russia, she will not be any threat to the world.

Russia will not invade Israel. Many teachers and writers have thought that the Gog and Magog of Ezekiel 38 represent Russia. This is not the case. Gog is Satan, and Magog is Satan's man on the earth. This is also true of Revelation 20 when Satan again as Gog and Magog marshalls

a great army against the Lord. That is his final
doom. Ezekiel 38, 39 and Revelation 20 depict similar situations—one before the return of Christ and
the other at the end of the Millennium. Antichrist's
first act when he comes into his kingdom will be
to destroy Russia as a world power.

It might seem that it would be easy to recognize Antichrist after all the things he does. His
getting control of many nations, his easy disposal
of Russia, his contact with the spirit world are all
identifying marks, but they will seem natural to
him. They will come in times of crisis, and most
people will not know the Scriptures.

There is no situation that will bring out more
clearly into the open the real character of the man
than his relationship to the Jews. His determination will be to annihilate every Jew. This will not
bring upon him an immediate punishment from
God. Instead God will use Antichrist to further
His purpose with Israel. God does not always
immediately punish His enemies. Sometimes He
uses them to fulfill His purpose. Antichrist's purpose will be to destroy Israel, but God's purpose
will be to use Antichrist to bring Israel back to
Him.

The prophets do not as a rule name Antichrist
in connection with the calamity that will befall
Israel, but it comes during the reign of Antichrist
and will probably be Antichrist's most conspicuous
identifying mark. What the prophets say will happen to Israel could not happen unless there was
a powerful man intent upon their destruction.
Isaiah calls Antichrist the Assyrian and says:

### ISAIAH 10
5 O Assyrian, the rod of mine anger, and the
staff in their hand is mine indignation.

6 I will send him against an hypocritical nation, and against the people of my wrath will

I give him a charge, to take the spoil, and to take the prey, and to tread them down like the mire of the streets.

7 Howbeit he meaneth not so, neither doth his heart think so; but it is in his heart to destroy and cut off nations not a few.

Daniel says that Antichrist will subdue three kings (nations) at the time of his rise to power. In Daniel the symbols of those nations are horns coming out of the head of the beast which is the Roman Empire. Daniel says that Antichrist will pull up three horns by the roots. Even at the start Antichrist will be a man of violence. This violence and expression of hatred will be especially evident in reference to the Jews. God will use Antichrist to bring the Jews to repentance. Then He will destroy Antichrist. This is expressed in the 12th verse of the 10th chapter of Isaiah:

ISAIAH 10

12 Wherefore it shall come to pass, that when the Lord hath performed his whole work upon mount Zion and on Jerusalem, I will punish the fruit of the stout heart of the king of Assyria, and the glory of his high looks.

When Antichrist comes into power, the first phase of the return of the Jews will have been completed, namely, the possession of the land. The next phase will be more difficult. No persecution ever turned the Jews back to God. Hitler succeeded only in causing some of them to return to the land.

Antichrist's persecution will be much more terrible than Hitler's. Hitler used gas chambers; he got rid of six million Jews, but Antichrist's purpose will be to do away with all Jews of all nations. That many Jews cannot be driven into gas chambers, but they could be driven into Egypt.

Egypt has great deserts where Jews could be sent
to die and their bones would not clutter up good
ground.

The nations who want to participate in the prosperous economy under Antichrist, and that would
be all of them, will have to cooperate in this vast
program of getting rid of all Jews. The program,
however, will not be completed until God acts in
a marvelous and miraculous way. God cannot act
to save the Jews until the Jews keep their end
of the covenant. This was expressed by Moses in
his last address to all Israel before he died.

### DEUTERONOMY 30

1 And it shall come to pass, when all these
things are come upon thee, the blessing and the
curse, which I have set before thee, and thou
shalt call them to mind among all the nations,
whither the Lord thy God hath driven thee,

2 And shalt return unto the Lord thy God,
and shalt obey his voice according to all that I
command thee this day, thou and thy children,
with all thine heart, and with all thy soul;

3 That then the Lord thy God will turn thy
captivity, and have compassion upon thee, and
will return and gather thee from all the nations,
whither the Lord thy God hath scattered thee.

4 If any of thine be driven out unto the out-
most parts of heaven, from thence will the Lord
thy God gather thee, and from thence will he
fetch thee:

5 And the Lord thy God will bring thee into
the land which thy fathers possessed, and thou
shalt possess it; and he will do thee good, and
multiply thee above thy fathers.

God's relationship to Israel is a covenant relationship. The Jews have broken the terms of
the covenant. Some of them have returned to the
land, but few of them have returned to God. Their

possession of the land is precarious; they will know
no peace or security until the covenant is again
in force. This will require a persecution far beyond
anything that the Jews have yet experienced.

As Isaiah suggests, God will use Antichrist, the
"Assyrian," to work out His purpose for Israel.
The hatred of Antichrist for the Jews will be almost
beyond imagination. It will be the worst situation
they have ever faced. Ezekiel tells it in these
words:

### EZEKIEL 20

33 As I live, saith the Lord God, surely with
a mighty hand, and with a stretched out arm,
and with fury poured out, will I rule over you:

34 And I will bring you out from the people,
and will gather you out of the countries wherein
ye are scattered, with a mighty hand, and with
a stretched out arm, and with fury poured out.

35 And I will bring you into the wilderness of
the people (desert of Egypt), and there will I
plead with you face to face.

36 Like as I pleaded with your fathers in the
wilderness of the land of Egypt, so will I plead
with you, saith the Lord God.

37 And I will cause you to pass under the rod,
and I will bring you into the bond of the covenant:

38 And I will purge out from among you the
rebels, and them that transgress against me: I
will bring them forth out of the country where
they sojourn, and they shall not enter into the land
of Israel: and ye shall know that I am the Lord.

When the Jews return to God, according to the
words of Moses, then they will again be brought
under the bond of the covenant. Then the covenant
will be effective again, and God will have to keep
His part. The final return of the Jews from Egypt
and from all the world will be a miraculous demonstration of God's power just as it was when
they came out of Egypt the first time.

ISAIAH 11

11  And it shall come to pass in that day, that
the Lord shall set his hand again the second
time to recover the remnant of his people, which
shall be left, from Assyria, and from Egypt, and
from Pathros, and from Cush, and from Elam,
and from Shinar, and from Hamath, and from the
islands of the sea.

12  And he shall set up an ensign for the nations, and shall assemble the outcasts of Israel,
and gather together the dispersed of Judah from
the four corners of the earth.

13  The envy also of Ephraim shall depart, and
the adversaries of Judah shall be cut off: Ephraim
shall not envy Judah, and Judah shall not vex
Ephraim.

14  But they shall fly upon the shoulders of
the Philistines toward the west; they shall spoil
them of the east together: they shall lay their
hand upon Edom and Moab; and the children of
Ammon shall obey them.

15  And the Lord shall utterly destroy the
tongue of the Egyptian sea; and with his mighty
wind shall he shake his hand over the river, and
shall smite it in the seven streams, and make men
go over dryshod.

16  And there shall be an highway for the remnant of his people, which shall be left, from
Assyria; like as it was to Israel in the day that
he came up out of the land of Egypt.

One of the last things that Moses did before
he died, was to call the Israelites together and
in a long speech tell them what would happen to
them if they were true to God, and what would
happen to them if they should forsake the Lord.
Moses said, "If thou wilt not hearken unto the
voice of the Lord thy God, to observe to do all
his commandments and his statutes which I command thee this day; . . . all these curses shall
come upon thee." Then Moses lists a long series
of curses that will overcome them if they forsake
the Lord.

## DEUTERONOMY 28

63 And it shall come to pass, that as the Lord rejoiced over you to do you good, and to multiply you; so the Lord will rejoice over you to destroy you, and to bring you to nought; and ye shall be plucked from off the land whither thou goest to possess it.

64 And the Lord shall scatter thee among all people, from the one end of the earth even unto the other; and there thou shalt serve other gods, which neither thou nor thy fathers have known, even wood and stone.

65 And among these nations shalt thou find no ease, neither shall the sole of thy foot have rest: but the Lord shall give thee there a trembling heart, and failing of eyes, and sorrow of mind:

66 And thy life shall hang in doubt before thee; and thou shalt fear day and night, and shalt have none assurance of thy life:

67 In the morning thou shalt say, Would God it were even! and at even thou shalt say, Would God it were morning! for the fear of thine heart wherewith thou shalt fear, and for the sight of thine eyes which thou shalt see.

68 And the Lord shall bring thee into Egypt again with ships, by the way whereof I spake unto thee, Thou shalt see it no more again: and there ye shall be sold unto your enemies for bondmen and bondwomen, and no man shall buy you.

*"They will return to Egypt again with ships."* You do not go to Egypt in ships from Palestine. That is a land journey. If they are going in ships, they are going from all parts of the world. Antichrist will attempt to make Egypt the burial ground for all Israel. Many will probably die, and it will look as if the entire nation were doomed. It is only then that the Jews will turn to God for help, and will again be brought under the terms of the covenant. The covenant is expressed over and over again in such words as:

GENESIS 17

7 And I will establish my covenant between
me and thee and thy seed after thee in their
generations for an everlasting covenant, to be a
God unto thee, and to thy seed after thee.

8 And I will give unto thee, and to thy seed
after thee, the land wherein thou art a stranger,
all the land of Canaan, for an everlasting possession; and I will be their God.

When the covenant is again in force, you will
see the greatest series of miracles since the de-
liverance from Egypt under the leadership of
Moses.

## Act Two—Return to God

The first act involved the land. A substantial
portion of the land was returned to productivity,
and it became an independent state for the first
time in over 2000 years. However, the Jews did
not keep their end of the covenant. There was
no national repentance or turning to God, either
on the part of those who returned or those who
remained in their adopted lands. Even the persecution under Hitler that cost six million Jewish
lives did not turn them to God. They must repent
as a nation and acknowledge that their troubles
are due to the fact that they forsook the Lord
and broke their part of the covenant. This will
take some doing.

The second act of this drama will probably be
one of the worst calamities the Jews have ever
experienced. Hitler caused some of them to return
to their land. It will take a greater than Hitler
to force the entire nation into repentance. Although
Antichrist is not usually mentioned by name in
these prophecies, he is always there behind the
curtain. In this connection Isaiah refers to him

as the Assyrian. When we consider that all the persecutions of the last 2000 years have not restored the Jews to their covenant relationship with God, we begin to see the size of the task that Antichrist will unwittingly perform. This feature of the reign of Antichrist is so pronounced and so vividly portrayed in the Bible that it will be an identifying mark. You will be able to recognize Antichrist by his treatment of the Jews because it will be so extreme in nature that it could not be surpassed.

It may be that the reason Antichrist does not appear more times in these prophecies is that he is merely the agent of Satan. Satan is desperate; he is like a stag at bay. The Second Coming of Christ is approaching when Satan will be bound for 1000 years and then cast into the lake of fire. Christ is coming as the King of the Jews and will set up an everlasting kingdom. His capital will be Jerusalem. If Satan can annihilate all Jews, he can prevent the Second Coming of Christ. Satan must kill all the Jews, not just a portion of them.

Ezekiel describes the plight of the Jews of that day by the symbol: the valley of dry bones. "And, lo, they were very dry" (Ezek. 37:2). Ezekiel asked the astonishing question: "Can these bones live?" The Jews will be in such a state that their return is described by Ezekiel as a resurrection from the dead.

### EZEKIEL 37

11 Then he said unto me, Son of man, these bones are the whole house of Israel: behold, they say, Our bones are dried, and our hope is lost: we are cut off for our parts [it is all over with us].

12 Therefore prophesy and say unto them, Thus saith the Lord God; Behold, O my people, I

will open your graves, and cause you to come up
out of your graves, and bring you into the land
of Israel.

13 And ye shall know that I am the Lord, when
I have opened your graves, O my people, and
brought you up out of your graves,

14 And shall put my spirit in you, and ye shall
live, and I shall place you in your own land:
then shall ye know that I the Lord have spoken
it, and performed it, saith the Lord.

From the standpoint of Antichrist they are
being driven out of their homes, but from the standpoint of God they are being brought out of all
nations where they have been scattered "with a
mighty hand, and with a stretched out arm, and
with fury poured out" (Ezek. 20:34).

Egypt will be the gathering place for many
of these Jews (Deut. 28:68). The Jews who are
now in Israel will be completely uprooted and scattered in all directions.

### ISAIAH 11

11 And it shall come to pass in that day, that
the Lord shall set his hand again the second
time to recover the remnant of his people, which
shall be left, from Assyria, and from Egypt, and
from Pathros, and from Cush, and from Elam,
and from Shinar, and from Hamath, and from
the islands of the sea.

"And it shall come to pass in that day [the
day of fulfilled prophecy] that the Lord shall set
his hand again the second time to recover the remnant of his people, which shall be left." This is
the second time that the Jews have gone back
to their land by the hand of the Lord. This is going
to be a miraculous proceeding from beginning to
end. The Jews will be in a helpless state, even
trying to sell themselves as slaves. Only a remnant
will be left after the terrible persecution. They
represent several countries:

*Assyria.* There are no Assyrians now. Antichrist is called the Assyrian by Isaiah. So Antichrist's empire may be called Assyria in prophecy.

*Egypt.* There are few, if any, Jews in Egypt now, but a great company will be there for some time before the return. The return will be by way of Egypt.

*Pathros and Cush.* Cush is Ethiopia. Pathros is north of Ethiopia, a part of Egypt or the Sudan. There are Jews in Ethiopia, the only known descendants of the priesthood. Haile Selassie, the former emperor of Ethiopia, is a Jew, a descendant of King Solomon. He claimed to have the original Ark of the Covenant, and there is a great deal of evidence that it is there, in the keeping of the priests.

*Elam and Shinar.* Shinar is the site of Ancient Babylon. Elam is east of Shinar. It is not an independent country now, but it will be—not only independent, but great. There are some amazing prophecies concerning it. It is in Shinar and Elam that the wealth of the world will center in those days, and naturally it would attract many Jews. Prophecy shows how great changes will take place in that part of the world.

*Hamath.* This points to territory north of Palestine which will be well developed during that time of world prosperity and which, therefore, will contain many Jews.

*Islands of the Sea.* This is an idiomatic expression often used to indicate far distant lands. The Jews will come from the four corners of the earth.

Isaiah gives a list of the places from which the Jews will return to Palestine when the great mass return suddenly occurs. Let us look at these places.

The first one mentioned is Assyria. There is no Assyria today. It was one of the first world empires, although in those days the empire was comparatively small. It was not unusual for a prophet to call a future empire for which he had no name, by the name of an historical empire. Assyria is sometimes used by the prophets to refer to a future combination of countries such as the Roman Empire. Antichrist is called the Assyrian so we might consider that his kingdom would be known in prophecy as Assyria. So we may assume that Assyria here is a name applying to the kingdom of Antichrist.

"Islands of the Sea" is a term used in prophecy to indicate nations unknown to the writer. It could cover nations of the whole world where there are Jews.

The other places mentioned—Egypt, Pathros, Cush, Elam, Shinar, and Hamath—form a circle around Israel. Except for Cush, there are no Jews in those countries today, yet Isaiah lists them as though they were full of Jews.

Antichrist will create a world movement against the Jews. They will be put into ships and dumped in the desert wastes of Egypt as Ezekiel says, "with fury poured out." This will take some time. There will be a long and furious program. The intensity and the cruelty of this program is hard to conceive. The Jews will be blamed for everything, and a hatred for them will be systematically engendered. The program will be to rid this world of Jews who will be pointed out as a source of all the evils in the world. Dumping them into the deserts of Egypt will not be a total success. The Jews will spread over Egypt. Isaiah says that five cities of Egypt will speak Hebrew (Isa. 19:18).

Toward the end of the program Antichrist will attack Israel and scatter the Jews in all directions. They will rush to the countries around Israel, and those lands that Isaiah mentions will suddenly become populated by Jews. It will be Antichrist, not the Arabs, who will force the Jews out of Israel, but the Arabs will do their part. Obadiah paints the picture graphically in these words:

### OBADIAH

10 For thy violence against thy brother Jacob shame shall cover thee, and thou shalt be cut off for ever.

11 In the day that thou stoodest on the other side, in the day that the strangers carried away captive his forces, and foreigners entered into his gates, and cast lots upon Jerusalem, even thou wast as one of them.

12 But thou shouldest not have looked on the day of thy brother in the day that he became a stranger; neither shouldest thou have rejoiced over the children of Judah in the day of their destruction; neither shouldest thou have spoken proudly in the day of distress.

13 Thou shouldest not have entered into the gate of my people in the day of their calamity; yea, thou shouldest not have looked on their affliction in the day of their calamity, nor have laid hands on their substance in the day of their calamity;

14 Neither shouldest thou have stood in the crossway, to cut off those of his that did escape; neither shouldest thou have delivered up those of his that did remain in the day of distress.

It is then that God himself goes into action. Ezekiel suggests that the Jews will be outside their land only a brief time before the great mass return. He says:

### EZEKIEL 36

6 Prophesy therefore concerning the land of Israel, and say unto the mountains, and to the hills, to the rivers, and to the valleys, Thus saith the Lord God; Behold, I have spoken in my

jealousy and in my fury, because ye have borne the shame of the heathen:

7 Therefore thus saith the Lord God; I have lifted up mine hand, Surely the heathen that are about you, they shall bear their shame.

8 But ye, O mountains of Israel, ye shall shoot forth your branches, and yield your fruit to my people of Israel; for they are at hand to come.

9 For, behold, I am for you, and I will turn unto you, and ye shall be tilled and sown:

10 And I will multiply men upon you, all the house of Israel, even all of it: and the cities shall be inhabited, and the wastes shall be builded.

When the return of the Jews comes in fulfillment of prophecy, they will all go back at once from the places where they have been scattered. They would not do this of their own accord because so many of them are so well satisfied in their adopted lands. God will use Antichrist to force the Jews to return. It will be a mass movement comparable to the exodus of the Israelites from Egypt.

This will be a defeat for Antichrist. Antichrist's attempt to destroy all the Jews will result in their being firmly established in their land. They will repent and turn to God, and God will perform miracles for them similar to the ones which occurred in connection with the exodus from Egypt. The return of the Jews will be miraculous from start to finish.

## Act III—Return to Christ

Now the prophecies concerning their relationship to God have been fulfilled. The last act involves their relationship to Christ, their Messiah. To cause the Jews to accept Christ as the one they crucified will be still more difficult, and will require more effort on the part of God. Again God will use Antichrist to accomplish His purpose.

After the Jews have returned to their land, established their nation and built their temple, they will go back into sin and unbelief. They will lose the protection of the covenant. Antichrist will have a wholesome respect for them, especially because of the presence of the Ark of the Covenant which will again rest on Mt. Zion.

In the meantime the resurrection (the Rapture) will have taken place. The resurrection involves both the dead and the living; the dead will be raised, and all the living who are saved by belief in Christ will be caught up with them, and their bodies transformed. At that time Satan will be cast out of heaven and down to the earth; he will need a body, the body of a man. Antichrist will be mysteriously killed, and Satan will bring him back to life, which will amount to the incarnation of Satan (Rev. 13).

Everything will change when Satan reigns in person on this earth. Christians will be persecuted unto death. All the Jews will be in Israel so Israel will become the final target of Satan. Revelation puts it in these words:

## REVELATION 16

13 And I saw three unclean spirits like frogs come out of the mouth of the dragon, and out of the mouth of the beast, and out of the mouth of the false prophet.

14 For they are the spirits of devils, working miracles, which go forth unto the kings of the earth and of the whole world, to gather them to the battle of that great day of God Almighty.

15 Behold, I come as a thief. Blessed is he that watcheth, and keepeth his garments, lest he walk naked, and they see his shame.

16 And he gathered them together into a place called in the Hebrew tongue Armageddon.

Armageddon, which is in the northern part of present-day Israel, is not the battleground; it is the place of mobilization of the armies of the world. The great battle is over the city of Jerusalem. Zechariah tells the story:

### ZECHARIAH 14

1 Behold, the day of the Lord cometh, and thy spoil shall be divided in the midst of thee.

2 For I will gather all nations against Jerusalem to battle; and the city shall be taken, and the houses rifled, and the women ravished; and half of the city shall go forth into captivity, and the residue of the people shall not be cut off from the city.

3 Then shall the Lord go forth, and fight against those nations, as when he fought in the day of battle.

4 And his feet shall stand in that day upon the mount of Olives, which is before Jerusalem on the east, and the mount of Olives shall cleave in the midst thereof toward the east and toward the west, and there shall be a very great valley; and half of the mountain shall remove toward the north, and half of it toward the south.

5 And ye shall flee to the valley of the mountains; for the valley of the mountains shall reach unto Azal: yea, ye shall flee, like as ye fled from before the earthquake in the days of Uzziah king of Judah: and the Lord my God shall come, and all the saints with thee.

## The Doom of Antichrist

In Revelation Antichrist is called the Beast. When Satan takes over his body, there are three individuals involved: Satan, Antichrist, and the False Prophet. Satan will attempt to duplicate the trinity of God; his will be a trinity of evil. Although Satan will exist on earth in the person of Antichrist, he will also have his own individual-

ity. At the Second Coming of Christ, Antichrist
(the Beast) and the False Prophet will be cast
alive into the lake of fire, and Satan will be
bound in the bottomless pit for 1000 years:

### REVELATION 19

17 And I saw an angel standing in the sun;
and he cried with a loud voice, saying to all the
fowls that fly in the midst of heaven, Come and
gather yourselves together unto the supper of
the great God;

18 That ye may eat the flesh of kings, and the
flesh of captains, and the flesh of mighty men,
and the flesh of horses, and of them that sit on
them, and the flesh of all men, both free and
bond, both small and great.

19 And I saw the beast, and the kings of the
earth, and their armies, gathered together to
make war against him that sat on the horse,
and against his army.

20 And the beast was taken, and with him the
false prophet that wrought miracles before him,
with which he deceived them that had received
the mark of the beast, and them that worshipped
his image. These both were cast alive into a lake
of fire burning with brimstone.

21 And the remnant were slain with the sword
of him that sat upon the horse, which sword pro-
ceeded out of his mouth: and all the fowls were
filled with their flesh.

# The Roman Empire

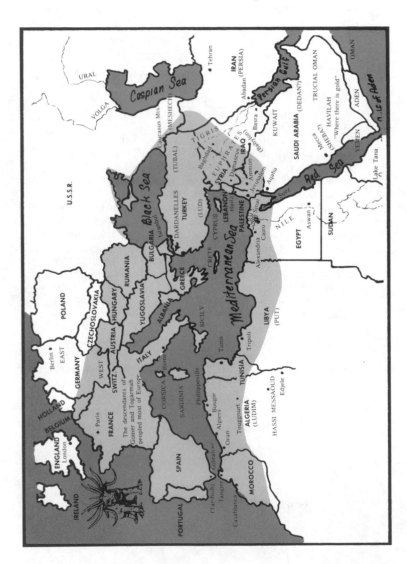

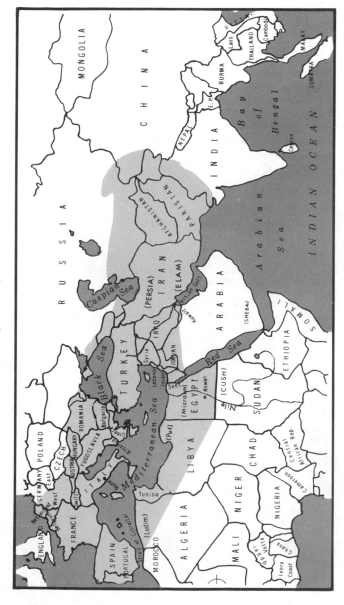

*The Empire of Antichrist*

## Books by Arthur E. Bloomfield

*ALL THINGS NEW* / A historical and eschatological interpretation of the book of Revelation emphasizing the futuristic and pre-millennial concept. Simply worded for maximum readability. $3.50.

*ALL THINGS NEW STUDY GUIDE* / Companion booklet for Bloomfield's book *All Things New*. 75¢.

*THE END OF THE DAYS* / A clear, easily readable explanation of the meaning of the prophecies of Daniel. $3.50.

*HOW TO RECOGNIZE THE ANTICHRIST* / A clear explanation of the Bible's description of the Man of Sin and his activities. $2.45.

*SIGNS OF HIS COMING* / An easy reading study of the Olivet Discourse. Helpful, structural, sequence charts included. $1.95.

*A SURVEY OF BIBLE PROPHECY* / A book which coordinates all the main events of prophecy in one single volume. The last chapter is a list of prophetic events in chronological order. With cyclopedic index. $2.95.

*BEFORE THE LAST BATTLE* / Identical to *A Survey of Bible Prophecy*, but without the cyclopedic index. Its colorful cover and exciting title makes the book an excellent gift to friends not yet greatly interested in prophecy. $2.25.